SEARCH
AND
DESTROY

ALSO BY HOWARD KORDER
Boys' Life and Other Plays

SEARCH AND DESTROY

A PLAY BY

Howard Korder

GROVE WEIDENFELD
New York

Published by Grove Weidenfeld
A division of Grove Press, Inc.
841 Broadway
New York, NY 10003-4793

Published in Canada by General Publishing Company, Ltd.

Library of Congress Cataloging-in-Publication Data

Korder, Howard.
Search and destroy : a play / by Howard Korder.—1st ed.
p.   cm.
ISBN 0-8021-3274-X (acid-free paper)
I. Title.
PS3561.06567S4   1992
812'.54—dc20   91-28951
                                                    CIP

Manufactured in the United States of America

Printed on acid-free paper

Designed by Irving Perkins Associates

First Edition 1992

First Evergreen Edition 1992

1   3   5   7   9   10   8   6   4   2

High? Man, I was flying; but not on the old gravy. It was the kind of high you get on when you've got to do something and can't. When you've got to have the answers and don't know any.

—JIM THOMPSON
A Hell of a Woman

The pure products of America
go crazy
—WILLIAM CARLOS WILLIAMS

Search and Destroy was presented by Yale Repertory Theater (Lloyd Richards, Artistic Director), opening on November 27, 1990. The cast, in order of appearance, was:

MARTIN MIRKHEIM	Joe Urla
ACCOUNTANT	Jarion Monroe
LAUREN	Claudia Feldstein
ROBERT	Anthony Forkush
JACKIE	Amy Povich
KIM	Keith Szarabajka
MARIE	Welker White
ROGER	Jeffrey Wright
HOTEL CLERK	William Francis McGuire
SECURITY GUARD	Christopher Bauer
DOCTOR WAXLING	Jarion Monroe
BUS DRIVER	Robert Beatty, Jr.
RON	Anthony Forkush
NUÑEZ	Michael Manuel
PAMFILO	José Zuniga
LEE	Thom Sesma
TERRY	Amy Povich
STATE TROOPER	Robert Beatty, Jr.
VOICE OF RADIO ANNOUNCER	Amy Povich
CARLING	William Francis McGuire

Search and Destroy was commissioned and originally produced by South Coast Repertory (David Emmes, Producing Artistic Director; Martin Benson, Artistic Director), opening on January 12, 1990. It was presented by *AT&T: On Stage* and was selected through the AT&T New Plays for the Nineties Project. The cast, in order of appearance, was:

MARTIN MIRKHEIM	Mark Harelik
ACCOUNTANT	Jarion Monroe
LAUREN	Anni Long
ROBERT	Anthony Forkush
JACKIE	Anni Long
KIM	Philip Anglim
VOICE OF FLIGHT ATTENDANT	Anni Long
MARIE	Dendrie Taylor
ROGER	Hubert Baron Kelly
HOTEL CLERK	Dom Magwili
SECURITY GUARD	Art Koustik
DOCTOR WAXLING	Jarion Monroe
BUS DRIVER	Vic Trevino
RON	Anthony Forkush
NUÑEZ	Art Koustik
PAMFILO	Vic Trevino
LEE	Dom Magwili
TERRY	Dendrie Taylor
STATE TROOPER	Hubert Baron Kelly
VOICE OF RADIO ANNOUNCER	Anni Long
CARLING	Jarion Monroe

Both productions were directed by David Chambers; the sets were by Chris Barreca; the costumes designed by Dunya Ramicova; the lighting designed by Chris Parry; the sound by David Budries; production photography by Joel Greenberg.

SEARCH
AND
DESTROY

Characters

MARTIN MIRKHEIM
ACCOUNTANT
LAUREN
ROBERT
JACKIE
KIM
MARIE
ROGER
HOTEL CLERK
SECURITY GUARD
DOCTOR WAXLING
BUS DRIVER
RON
NUÑEZ
PAMFILO
LEE
TERRY
STATE TROOPER
RADIO ANNOUNCER
CARLING

Time

The Present

Place

The United States of America

As the house lights dim.

WAXLING'S VOICE (*over speakers*): I get letters. Yes I do. People with problems. "Doctor Waxling, I see you on television . . . Doctor Waxling I am *confused*, Doctor Waxling I'm in *trouble*, I turn to *you* . . . as a last resort." To me. A message for these viewers. I hope they're watching. I'm only saying it once. "I'm trapped by my limitations," there *are* no limitations, ANYTHING IS POSSIBLE. "I can't escape the past," the past is *dead*, THROW IT AWAY. "I'm *worried*. I don't feel *safe*. I *want* to change but I'm *frightened* by my OWN WEAKNESS." Is that *you*? Is that your "problem"? Then I tell you *what*. You better be strong. It's that simple. *You . . . better . . . be . . . strong.*

ACT ONE

Scene 1

An office. MARTIN *in a chair,* ACCOUNTANT *seated behind desk.*

MARTIN: Okay. This . . .

(*Pause.*)

> Here is my plan. I see myself as, uh, I feel, I think my *abilities* . . . I hate fear. Hate it. Fear that makes you . . . that *stops* you. From realizing your . . . yourself. *Your . . . self.* What you *are.* What you know you could *be.* Because of that fear? No.

(*Pause.* ACCOUNTANT *shifts his papers.*)

> And this is not, "Hey, make me king," or, um, "Why can't *I* sleep with cover girls," because people who, that's not an *ambition.* That's . . . they don't *know* anything. The world, themselves . . . they waste their energies. On . . . what? It's foolish. Have a purpose. A *serious* purpose. Because . . . okay. Here we are, planet Earth, boom. What's important? A neat desk? "He was kind to children"? No. "I will *die* one day so let me leave something behind." Something *good.* Something *lasting.* Something of myself. Let them know I was here. Let them *know* I was here. Let them know.

(*He looks at the* ACCOUNTANT. *Pause.*)

ACCOUNTANT: You owe the state of Florida thirty-seven thousand nine hundred and fifty-six dollars.

MARTIN: Uh-huh. Okay.

ACCOUNTANT: Exclusive of interest and penalties.

MARTIN: I understand *your* position—

ACCOUNTANT: You failed to file or substantially underpaid corporate taxes for the first fiscal quarter of 1990, the second fiscal quarter of 1990, the fourth fiscal quarter of 1990, and the first fiscal quarter of 1991. That is as Mirkheim Enterprises, Incorporated, doing business variously as Startime Booking, Big Top Tours, and the Southern Skating Spectacular. You are listed as sole proprietor of Mirkheim Enterprises, is that correct?

MARTIN: I'm trying to explain, my intentions—

ACCOUNTANT: I need to know if that's correct, Mister Mirkheim.

(*Pause.*)

MARTIN: Yes.

ACCOUNTANT: In the last quarter you filed, you claimed—

MARTIN: My corporation—

ACCOUNTANT: *Corporation* claimed as operating expenses the mortgage and maintenance on a condominium apartment in Boca Raton. This apartment is also listed as your place of residence.

MARTIN: Okay, *first*, I work at home so—

ACCOUNTANT: You claim payment of twenty-two thousand dollars to a Ms. Lauren Mirkheim as a nonexclusive consultant to your firm. We are interested in the nature of her services.

MARTIN: She happens to hold a business degree from—

ACCOUNTANT: We are interested in seeing your records. We are interested in your *corporation's* income during the last year. We are very interested in determining—

MARTIN: What's your point.

(*Pause.*)

Please.

ACCOUNTANT: You owe the state of Florida thirty-seven thousand nine hundred fifty-six dollars. Exclusive of interest and penalties.

(*Pause.*)

MARTIN: What if I don't have it?

ACCOUNTANT: The state of Florida is legally empowered to place a lien upon your holdings, both real and intangible, and initiate criminal proceedings. We do not like to be taken advantage of, Mister Mirkheim.

MARTIN: I was not taking advantage, sir, I—

ACCOUNTANT: How would you describe it?

(*Pause.*)

MARTIN: It's outside my main focus.

ACCOUNTANT: Your *main* focus.

MARTIN: The area of my concern.

ACCOUNTANT: Which is.

MARTIN: I've been *telling* you.

ACCOUNTANT: You're frightened of dying, was that it?

MARTIN: No, please *listen*. I *know* how this looks. I *know* why I'm here.

ACCOUNTANT: Why are you here.

MARTIN: I am here . . . because I haven't paid as much attention recently to—

ACCOUNTANT: That's not exactly—

MARTIN: —attention as I should have to something you
      seem to . . . something important. It's important. I've
      let it go too long, that's a bad mistake. Now whatever
      my debts are I'll honor them. I give you my word. All I
      ask, simple request, not to be bullied, not to be threat-
      ened. I'm speaking to you openly because I believe
      there's a better way to be. So when I say I'm trying to
      achieve something, and haven't had time to attend to
      every—

ACCOUNTANT: You're a young man, Mister Mirkheim.

MARTIN: Can I just—

ACCOUNTANT: You're a young man with a healthy income and
      a bad attitude toward reporting it. I suggest you *make*
      time for matters of more pressing import.

MARTIN: Such as?

ACCOUNTANT: Thirty-seven thousand nine hundred—

MARTIN: No, now you're— Is that supposed to *scare* me? I
      owe *money*? Some *numbers*? You think that's what
      counts?

ACCOUNTANT: It might warrant *my* respect.

MARTIN: I bet it would.

ACCOUNTANT: Excuse me?

MARTIN: You'd be down on your knees shaking. You'd be
      sobbing to Jesus.

(*Pause.*)

ACCOUNTANT: You owe us, Mister Mirkheim. It's time to
      pay. This office will be in touch with you shortly. You
      might find the services of a lawyer useful.

MARTIN: I don't need one.

ACCOUNTANT: Your expertise is vast.

MARTIN: Are we done?

ACCOUNTANT: For now.

MARTIN: Let me tell you something.

ACCOUNTANT: Mmm-hmm.

MARTIN: This country . . .

(*The* ACCOUNTANT *looks away.*)

    Excuse me . . .

(*The* ACCOUNTANT *looks at him.*)

ACCOUNTANT: Yes?

MARTIN: . . . is about *possibilities*.

ACCOUNTANT: I'll keep that in mind, Mister Mirkheim. Have a nice day.

Scene 2

A sun deck. LAUREN *on chaise longue in bathing suit,* MARTIN, *in suit and tie, on top of her.*

LAUREN (*after a moment*): Marty.

(*Pause.*)

    Marty.

MARTIN: Yes.

LAUREN: Please.

MARTIN: What.

LAUREN: Don't fuck me on the sun deck.

(*Pause.*)

MARTIN: Why not?

LAUREN: I don't *want* you to.

(*Pause.*)

MARTIN: Let's go inside.

LAUREN: No.

MARTIN: Come on.

LAUREN: The cleaning lady's there.

MARTIN: She won't see us.

LAUREN: Marty. *Marty.*

(*Pause.*)

We're not doing any more of this. It's *over.* Okay?

(*Pause.* MARTIN *stands up.*)

I thought you were trying celibacy.

MARTIN: I am.

LAUREN: You should try harder.

MARTIN: I should. I'm going to. I *will.*

(*Pause. He picks up a book lying by the chaise.*)

Still on the same chapter.

LAUREN: It's a long book.

MARTIN: He says some very important things in here.

LAUREN: Well.

MARTIN: About the world. How to live.

LAUREN: Since when do you read?

MARTIN: Since now.

LAUREN: I just can't get into it.

MARTIN: He's on TV every week. You could watch with me.

LAUREN: Let's not start.

MARTIN: We could be together.

LAUREN: Marty, make up your mind.

MARTIN: I *want* us together. I wanted us to *change* together.

LAUREN: I'm happy the way I am.

MARTIN: Everyone says that.

LAUREN: I know it. I know how *I* feel.

MARTIN: You do too much coke.

LAUREN: Well thank God I never saw you trying to suck your face off a mirror.

MARTIN: I'm done with all that.

LAUREN: I forgot, you're a new man.

MARTIN: I'm trying to be.

LAUREN: We're not kids now, Marty.

MARTIN: That's exactly *why*.

LAUREN: So walk out on me, give up a good business—

MARTIN: No, no, I didn't "give it up," I—

LAUREN: Running around the country five years, finally I think I get to stay in one—

MARTIN: Lauren, Lauren, *listen* to me, the business was nothing. Circus tours. Booking wrestlers. Polka bands. It proved nothing. What is *that*. What have I *done*.

LAUREN: What've you done, you have a condo, you have—

MARTIN: No. Not *things*. Deeds. I'm talking about deeds.

(*Pause.*)

LAUREN: My lawyer thinks you shouldn't be here.

MARTIN: I'm going.

LAUREN: I'm sorry I have to say that.

MARTIN: I have an appointment anyway.

LAUREN: And you'll take care of that check.

MARTIN: Yeah, I, just forgot to transfer the money. It'll clear this time.

(*Pause.*)

Can you wait a week, ten days?

LAUREN: Again?

MARTIN: Last time. I promise. There's a project I'm working on. Something I care about. When it's done everything'll be different.

LAUREN: Will it.

MARTIN: Yes. I wish you could understand that.

(*Pause.*)

LAUREN: Alright.

MARTIN: Thank you.

(*He offers her the book.*)

Here.

LAUREN: It's okay.

MARTIN: I can get another copy.

LAUREN: I'm done with the book, Marty.

(*Pause.*)

What is it?

MARTIN: Hmm?

LAUREN: What's your project?

(MARTIN *looks out front. Pause.*)

MARTIN: You can see clear to the horizon from here.

Scene 3

A terrace. Evening. MARTIN *in his suit.* ROBERT *in casual wear. Sounds of a party from inside.*

ROBERT: Where'd it go, Marty?

MARTIN: I don't know, Rob.

ROBERT: Where'd all that money *go*, you know? I mean Jesus. Six hundred points they're saying "no cause for alarm." *Fuck* me.

(*Pause.*)

MARTIN: How much did you lose?

ROBERT: A lot. Boodles. Great entire boodles. Fuck fuck why didn't I see this coming? Why am I throwing this *party.*

MARTIN: You'll make it back.

ROBERT: Will I.

(*Pause.*)

How'd you come out?

MARTIN: I'm not too worried.

ROBERT: You're not.

MARTIN: It's just, you know, the economy.

ROBERT: Just that, huh?

MARTIN: Yeah.

ROBERT: God bless you, Marty.

(JACKIE, *Robert's wife, enters. She sees* MARTIN.)

JACKIE: Oh. (*To* ROBERT:) Are you spending the whole evening out here?

ROBERT: I'd like to enjoy my terrace before I jump off it.

JACKIE: It's your friends in there, not mine.

ROBERT: Honey, I kinda lost several hundred thousand dollars today. Be nice to me.

MARTIN: Hello, Jackie.

JACKIE: Yes.

(*She exits. Pause.*)

MARTIN: She's mad at me.

ROBERT: Well, you know, Lauren's calling her.

MARTIN: Yah.

ROBERT: What do you want, they're sisters.

(*Pause.*)

  Tell you what my broker says.

MARTIN: What.

ROBERT: Fear.

MARTIN: What about it?

ROBERT: He thinks it's going to be big. He thinks we're gonna be hearing a lot from fear in the nineties. It's going to be the fear *decade*. And he says . . .

(KIM *walks onto the terrace.* ROBERT *drops his voice.*)

He says now's the time to ground-floor it.

MARTIN: Fear?

ROBERT: Fear-related industries. Blood analyzers. Viral filters. UV screens. Toteable security systems. Impact-proof leisurewear, I've seen that. I mean, this is you walk into K Mart, you go buy something makes you feel safe. Very cutting edge, very hot. Which sounds great except here I am stuck with my pants around my ankles three hundred K in the hole. Majorly sucks.

(*Pause. Party noise from inside.*)

MARTIN (*producing book*): You read this, Rob?

ROBERT (*not looking at it*): Wish I had time, Marty.

MARTIN: You should.

ROBERT: What's it, the new Trump thing? Dead meat, kid, dead meat.

MARTIN: No, he talks about all this stuff. And what it *means*.

ROBERT: Who does?

MARTIN: Doctor Waxling.

ROBERT: I'm sorry?

MARTIN: Luther Waxling. Who wrote the book.

(*Pause.*)

ROBERT: Guy on cable three in the morning?

MARTIN: Yes.

ROBERT: Staying up late, buddy boy. (*Looking at cover.*) *Daniel Strong.*

MARTIN: Right.

ROBERT: Looks interesting.

MARTIN: No, you're only saying, but it is.

ROBERT: I'm sure.

MARTIN: He, what he does, it's the story of this young, Daniel, Strong, it starts, he's born—

ROBERT: Uh-huh.

MARTIN: And he grows up in this, the world, where the system, the schools and everything, it, it *crushes* him, inside, they teach him to be worthless—

ROBERT: Yeah, right.

MARTIN: And then, as a man, he goes on a jour—an *adventure,* during which, he discovers within *himself* the power—

(JACKIE *enters.*)

JACKIE: Your business partner's doing lines in the playroom.

ROBERT: Shit.

JACKIE: We agreed no drugs tonight.

ROBERT: He was clean at the door.

JACKIE: Well he scored off somebody.

ROBERT: Yeah, I'll, okay.

(JACKIE *exits.*)

    Marty, excuse me.

MARTIN: I just want to tell you about this.

ROBERT: Sounds great, really—

MARTIN: Yeah, so, I want to *do* something with it.

ROBERT: Huh?

MARTIN: I want to buy the book, the rights to the book, and do something with it.

ROBERT: You want to . . .

MARTIN: Buy the rights. Make a movie.

(*Pause.* ROBERT *laughs.*)

What's funny?

ROBERT: "Mirkheim Studios Presents . . ."

MARTIN: So?

(ROBERT *keeps laughing.*)

Why not?

ROBERT: No, good luck.

MARTIN: You think I can't do it?

ROBERT: I . . . It's not like booking Smurfs on Ice, Mart.

MARTIN: I'm aware of that.

ROBERT: You see good money, Mart. What do you want, respect?

MARTIN: I want to *achieve* something—

ROBERT: Bad time for that, boyo. Trust me. *Good* time for sticking to what you know and holding on to what you got, yes?

MARTIN: No, 'cause by applying my *abilities*—

ROBERT: Mart. Honestly. Honestly now. Let's not . . . *over-estimate*, huh? Who we are?

MARTIN: What are you saying?

ROBERT: I'm saying . . . what am I saying, you been lucky. It was easy pickings these last few years and we've *all* been very lucky. But top of the food chain you're not.

(*Pause.*)

And I *speak* this out of love.

MARTIN: I thought you could help me.

ROBERT: What I'm doing.

MARTIN: Not like this.

ROBERT: You want money? I can't *give* you money. I set you
up once, I can't do that now.

MARTIN: I don't want money. I want contacts. You know
people.

ROBERT: I know *some* people.

MARTIN: So put me in touch with them.

(*Pause.*)

ROBERT: Did you *talk* to the guy?

MARTIN: Which.

ROBERT: The book guy.

MARTIN: Not yet.

ROBERT: So if you can buy the thing you don't even know.

(*Pause.*)

    Marty? Right?

MARTIN: It's not a problem.

ROBERT: Why's that.

MARTIN: Because when I meet him he'll see.

ROBERT: What, that you floss nightly?

MARTIN: That I understand what he's talking about. (*Pause.*)
It's time to change, Rob. Don't you *feel* that? We all
have to *change*.

(ROBERT *looks at him. Pause.* JACKIE *enters and stands
there.*)

ROBERT: O*kay.*

(*He turns and starts off with her. To* MARTIN:)

    Call me later.

MARTIN: Does that mean you'll help?

ROBERT: It means call me later.

(*They exit.* MARTIN *looks out. Silence.*)

KIM: People waste their time.

MARTIN: Pardon?

KIM: They waste their time. They make excuses, they consider the fine points, they start arguments. Factors arise. Moments pass. Directions are mislaid. We sit in the car. We wonder where we were going, and why we had to get there. You smoke?

MARTIN: No.

KIM: I do. Helps me think. You mind?

(MARTIN *shakes his head.* KIM *lights a cigarette.*)

Get evenings like this in the Mediterranean.

MARTIN: Do you?

KIM: Oh yes.

(*Pause.*)

MARTIN (*offering his hand*): Martin Mirkheim.

KIM: Kim Feston.

MARTIN: You're not a friend of Rob's?

KIM: No.

MARTIN: I didn't think so.

(*Pause.*)

KIM: And are you in business, Martin?

MARTIN: Well, I . . . yes.

KIM: I say this: God bless the businessmen.

MARTIN: Why's that.

KIM: They are the . . . *agents* of our hope.

MARTIN: Huh.

(*Pause.*)

That's a lovely phrase.

KIM: You appreciate language.

MARTIN: I'm not good at it myself . . .

KIM: But you're keen to the possibilities.

MARTIN: It just strikes me a certain way.

KIM: You are not a modern man.

(*Pause.*)

MARTIN: And yourself?

KIM: Yes?

MARTIN: Are you in business?

KIM: On occasion.

MARTIN: Ah.

KIM: In a freelance capacity. With an overseas consultancy firm. Mostly based in New York.

MARTIN: What brings you here?

KIM: Doing some work. For your friend's partner, I *think*.

MARTIN: Sounds interesting.

KIM: Well.

(*Pause. They look at each other.*)

I've read that, you know.

MARTIN: *Daniel Strong?*

KIM: Uh-huh.

MARTIN: You're kidding.

KIM: No. It had a . . . powerful effect on me.

MARTIN: Really.

KIM: Oh yes. That scene on the mountaintop.

MARTIN: Hmm, he's all alone, he's lost, starving . . .

KIM: The sun begins to rise, the city stretched out far below . . .

MARTIN: He remembers the day he killed his father.

KIM: He hears a voice—

MARTIN: His *own* voice saying what?

KIM: "There was nothing to be forgiven. And anything was possible."

MARTIN: Right. Right.

KIM: The best book when you're nineteen.

(*Pause.*)

MARTIN: I'm going to make a movie of it.

KIM: Yes. I overheard. What a superb idea.

MARTIN: You're not in the . . . film—

KIM: No.

MARTIN: Sorry.

KIM: Oh, don't apologize. We don't have to do that.

(*He smiles.* ROBERT *enters with* JACKIE *behind him. Pause.*)

ROBERT: Uh . . . yeah. Um . . .

(*Pause.*)

Look. I'm really sorry about this. I'm gonna . . . I'm afraid I'm gonna have to ask you to, ah, to leave my house. I'm sorry.

(*Pause.*)

KIM: Are you speaking to me?

ROBERT: Yah.

(*Pause.*)

KIM: Why?

JACKIE: You know why.

(KIM *and* JACKIE *look at each other. Pause.*)

KIM: Thank you for having me. You spread a lovely buffet.

JACKIE: You're welcome.

KIM (*to* MARTIN): We should talk more. If you're ever in New
     York . . . give me a call. I mean that.

(*He hands* MARTIN *a business card and exits.* MARTIN
watches him go, then turns to ROBERT *and* JACKIE.)

MARTIN: What . . . ?

(ROBERT *gestures "don't ask" and starts walking away.* MAR-
     TIN *stops him.*)

     Rob. I'll do it myself.

ROBERT: Huh?

MARTIN: I'm going to do it myself.

(ROBERT *looks at him. Pause.*)

ROBERT: This fucking *day* . . .

Scene 4

Another office. MARIE, *the receptionist, behind desk.* MAR-
TIN *standing before her with a small bandage on his temple.*

MARTIN: I'd like to see Doctor Waxling.

MARIE: Is he expecting you?

MARTIN: Oh yes.

MARIE: Your name, please?

MARTIN: Martin Mirkheim.

MARIE: Thank you.

(*She picks up phone.*)

Mister Mirkheim to see Doctor Waxling.

(*Pause.*)

He says so, yes.

(*Pause. To* MARTIN:)

May I ask what this is in reference to?

MARTIN: It's a personal matter.

MARIE (*into phone*): He says it's personal.

(*Pause. To* MARTIN:)

He'll be right with you.

MARTIN: He will. Thank you.

(*Pause.*)

Is the show taped here in Dallas?

MARIE: Huh?

MARTIN: Doctor Waxling's show, taped in the building?

MARIE: No. The station.

MARTIN: Of course.

MARIE: These are the Waxling Institute's international headquarters.

MARTIN: Ah.

(*Silence.* ROGER *enters in business suit.*)

ROGER: Hello.

MARTIN: Hi.

ROGER: I'm Roger.

MARTIN: Yes. Alright.

ROGER: You wanted to see Doctor Waxling.

MARTIN: Correct.

ROGER: That's not possible right now.

MARTIN: Why?

ROGER: He's busy.

MARTIN: I see.

ROGER: Perhaps I can help you.

MARTIN: It's a personal matter.

ROGER: Of what nature?

MARTIN: A personal nature.

(*Pause.*)

ROGER: Well, we're very happy you've walked in, sir. Getting personal is what we're about.

MARTIN: Thank you.

ROGER: You should know that Doctor Waxling requests applicants first complete the Mastery Sessions before individual consultation. A lot of what he says is based on exposure to the introductory material. Now I'd be happy to set up an appointment with one of our—

MARTIN: Who are you?

ROGER: Excuse me?

MARTIN: Who *are* you?

ROGER: I'm Roger. I'm Doctor Waxling's assistant.

MARTIN: Roger. Okay. I'm not here for that. Would you please tell him that Martin Mirkheim wants to see him. I am president of Mirkheim Enterprises, Incorporated.

I have flown here directly from Florida and I have something very important to discuss with him.

ROGER: What would that company be, sir?

MARTIN: Mirkheim Enterprises is a diversified organization focused primarily in the field of entertainment.

ROGER: I'm not familiar with it.

MARTIN: We're a prominent presence in the southeastern states.

ROGER: Ah.

MARTIN: I own, my company owns, several television stations in Florida and, *Georgia*, WKRG there, we also have interests, are *active in*, the, area, of motion picture production, which, maybe you've heard, it's primed for very very explosive growth on the peninsula with heavy involvement from the major studios.

ROGER: I wasn't aware of that.

MARTIN: Yes, very exciting. We're about to enter into an agreement with Twentieth Cent— legally I shouldn't say, and, ah, unfortunately I have a busy schedule in Dallas, leaving tomorrow, I'm meeting very shortly with some petroleum people, if Doctor Waxling wishes to talk I'm afraid it's going to have to be in the next half-hour.

(*Pause.*)

ROGER: And that would be in reference to . . .

MARTIN: The matter I've mentioned.

ROGER: The personal matter.

MARTIN: Yes.

(*Pause.*)

ROGER: I'm sorry sir, you're out of luck. Doctor Waxling is taping all day.

MARTIN: Ah, Roger. Yes. That's very good. I realize you're just doing your job, but—

ROGER: Sir, I've told you—

MARTIN: I don't think you quite understand what—

ROGER: No. No, I do understand, sir. I do. You want to see the Doctor. You can't. I will certainly tell him you stopped *in* . . . and I hope you enjoy your stay in Dallas.

MARTIN: Listen, your behavior—

ROGER: Mister Mirkheim. This building has an excellent security staff.

MARTIN: It does.

ROGER: Yes.

(*Pause.*)

Good-bye.

(*He shakes Martin's hand and exits. Pause.* MARTIN *rises and turns to* MARIE.)

MARTIN: How come no one here has an accent?

MARIE: You mean like a Texas accent?

MARTIN: Yah.

MARIE: Well, you know. Everybody's from everywhere.

MARTIN: Hum.

(*Pause.*)

Was he someone important?

MARIE: He thinks so.

(*Pause.*)

You're a producer?

MARTIN: Pardon?

MARIE: A movie producer?

MARTIN: Yes. That *is* what I am.

MARIE: Huh, what kind movies?

MARTIN: Various . . . kinds.

MARIE: Like slasher stuff?

MARTIN: No.

MARIE: People talking ones.

MARTIN: I suppose.

MARIE: Those are okay.

MARTIN: Well.

MARIE: Anything I would know?

(*Pause.*)

MARTIN: Did you see *Pretty Woman*?

MARIE: Yuh.

MARTIN: I was involved on that.

MARIE: Huh.

(*Pause.*)

    Bang your head?

MARTIN: Sorry?

MARIE: Your head.

MARTIN: Oh. No.

(*Pause.*)

    Well.

(*He starts out.*)

MARIE: Could I send you one?

MARTIN: Send me what?

MARIE: One I wrote. A script.

MARTIN: Ah.

MARIE: Yeah, I took a class, I mean, why not, right? 'Cause I *have* ideas.

MARTIN: Right.

MARIE: Could, would you mind if I did?

(*Pause.*)

MARTIN: What's your name?

MARIE: Marie.

MARTIN: Marie. Hi. Listen—

MARIE: I know, send it to your whatever.

MARTIN: No. No, I don't work that way, Marie. I don't treat people like that. I would like to hear about your script.

MARIE: Really.

MARTIN: I *can't* right now.

MARIE: Sure, thanks.

MARTIN: I'm leaving tomorrow. I could— No, I'm sorry.

MARIE: What?

MARTIN: No, it wouldn't sound right. Send me your script.

MARIE: What wouldn't?

MARTIN: I'm free tonight, but to—

MARIE: You want me to come to your hotel.

(*Pause.*)

    Right?

MARTIN: *My* hotel. Ah.

(*Pause.*)

Yah, sure. Why don't you do that. I'm at the Omni
Atrium. It's over by—

MARIE: It's right by the airport.

MARTIN: Yes. Exactly.

MARIE: There's a restaurant there. If you want to eat.

MARTIN: The hotel? Of course. I hope you'll be my guest.

MARIE: I mean in the airport.

(*Pause.*)

MARTIN: Well, that's fine too.

MARIE: Okay.

(*Pause.*)

    I know something you don't.

MARTIN: What?

MARIE: There's blood on you.

MARTIN: Where?

(*She points at his tie.* MARTIN *lifts it up to reveal a half-dollar-size spot of blood.* MARIE *touches it with her finger.*)

MARIE: It's still wet.

(*She holds up her finger.* MARTIN *looks at it. The phone rings twice.*)

Scene 5

An airport snack bar. MARTIN *holding bound script,* MARIE
sitting opposite.

MARIE: Everybody's dead all over. Okay. She's caught. The spinesucker has her pinned against the wall. With his other hand he cracks open her boyfriend's head and smears his brains all over her tits. Okay. The elevator's stuck between floors. This thing comes out of him like a gangrene penis with a lobster claw and starts burrowing into her. The pain's unbearable. Okay. Finally she manages to reach the switch on the radial saw and rips it into him. But he just smiles, okay, his stomach opens up and he absorbs it, like he does and goes on pumping her up. She's gonna die, that's all. *Except* inside him the saw's still going, spinning around, he starts shaking and there's a, what do you, close shot, yeah, and the saw rips out of his chest, there's this explosion of meat and pus pouring out like from a fire hose, he climbs on her and tries to shove the penis claw down her throat, okay, but she hacks it off with the saw okay he goes shooting back against the glass door okay they break he falls five floors, onto the metal spike in the fountain it goes straight through his face, his brains spurt out and slide into the water like fresh cum okay. He's dead, he's dead, he's finally fucking dead. She walks away that's the end.

(*Pause.*)

MARTIN: And this is your *first* script.

MARIE: No. I wrote one in class.

MARTIN: Ah.

(*Pause.*)

     The same sort of—?

MARIE: Horror, yeah, I like the horror.

MARTIN: Mmm.

MARIE: Makes you feel something.

MARTIN: Yes.

(*Pause.*)

It's very violent.

MARIE: You wouldn't do that?

MARTIN: I might.

MARIE: How much would you pay me for it?

MARTIN: That depends.

MARIE: Half a million dollars?

MARTIN: I have to read it first.

MARIE: Sure.

(*Pause.*)

MARTIN: How's the burger?

MARIE: Okay.

MARTIN: They just leave them sitting under heat lamps all day.

MARIE: I don't come here for the food.

(*Pause.*)

MARTIN: You from Dallas, Marie?

MARIE: Cincinnati.

MARTIN: What's that like?

MARIE: This. Basically like this.

MARTIN: How long you been working for the Doctor.

MARIE: Few months.

MARTIN: Have much to do with him?

MARIE: Sometimes. Sometimes much.

MARTIN: Tough man to get to.

MARIE: You shoulda made an appointment first.

MARTIN: There was a little mix-up.

MARIE: I would of let you in, but Roger . . .

MARTIN: He seems very dedicated.

MARIE: Two tabs Dexedrine he thinks he's Mighty Mouse. You told him you know the Doctor?

MARTIN: Well, I don't like to throw names around. We'll get it all straightened out tomorrow.

MARIE: You're seeing the Doctor tomorrow?

MARTIN: I do have other business, but possibly I could squeeze—

MARIE: 'Cause I think he's starting a lecture tour tomorrow.

MARTIN: What?

MARIE: Yeah, he's gonna be in Minneapolis.

MARTIN: Minneapolis.

MARIE: Right. In Minnesota.

(*Pause.*)

Are you alright?

MARTIN: Oh yes. I'm fine. He told me, of course. I forgot. Minneapolis.

MARIE: Big trip for nothing, huh.

MARTIN: For nothing, no, I met you, I have, there's your *script*, ah, *Dead World* . . .

MARIE: My teacher says it's not a good title.

MARTIN: Oh no, very eye-catching.

MARIE: Thanks.

(*Silence. Jet takes off.* MARIE *follows it with her eyes. Pause.*)

That's the last plane for two hours.

MARTIN: They'll probably want to close up.

MARIE: You can sit here all night, they don't care.

MARTIN: Is that what you're going to do?

MARIE: I don't know.

MARTIN: Well, I better get back. I'm up early tomorrow, some big meetings in town before I fly out.

MARIE: Okay.

(*Pause.*)

Kye ask you a question?

MARTIN: Of course.

MARIE: How come you lie so much?

MARTIN: What?

MARIE: You lie a lot.

(*Pause.*)

MARTIN: How do you mean?

MARIE: Um . . . the office this afternoon you lied you had an appointment, you said some stuff to Roger I don't know sounded kinda stupid you told me the Doctor knows you maybe he does I don't think so. And the other stuff about the movies and everything, I kinda wonder about, 'cause the movies, that's California, you're in Dallas, you're sitting in the airport snack bar and you're talking to *me*. And I'm not anybody.

MARTIN: Uh-huh.

MARIE: So that's a lot of lying in the time I know you, which isn't very long.

(*Pause.*)

MARTIN: Does that bother you?

MARIE: It might. I lie. I don't do it right. I lie at the end when I'm scared and I don't get anything. You're lying at the beginning. What do you want to get?

(*Pause.*)

MARTIN: Marie.

MARIE: Yah.

MARTIN: I need your help.

MARIE: What for?

MARTIN: I *have* to get to Doctor Waxling. I flew here from Florida. I'll fly to Minneapolis, I don't care. I have to reach him.

MARIE: Why?

MARTIN: Because . . . alright. Yes. I lied, I lied, I did. I'm a liar. I don't want to be. I *want* to be true. To make myself *become* true. But it's so hard, Marie. You know what I'm saying?

MARIE: You're not a movie producer.

MARTIN: That's not the point—

MARIE: Are you?

MARTIN: No I'm not. I mean I *am.* I *am* a producer. No, I *haven't* made a movie. So what. So *what*, right? I am what I say I am because what . . . what you say you *are*, that's what you'll be.

MARIE: Just by saying it.

MARTIN: Okay. Okay. I understand. You're thinking, what is he, he lures me here, no, lures me, he's promising things, my script, get me into *bed* . . . alright. I *admit* it. There it is. But . . . but . . . listen to me. Do you believe in anything?

MARIE: Do I . . . ?

MARTIN: Believe. In anything.

(*Pause.*)

MARIE: Not especially.

MARTIN: I do. Now this is true. I *do* believe. I believe in myself. I believe in my power to affect things. And if you help me, you will have that power too. I need to meet the Doctor. I *need* to get his book. The rights to his book *Daniel Strong*. That means something to me. It *means* something. I know you feel that. I know you *understand* what I'm saying. I know it.

(*Pause.*)

MARIE: If you went to Minneapolis . . .

MARTIN: I will do that. Yes. Then what?

MARIE: What I could do is get you a pass. For backstage. You just walk through.

MARTIN: And then I would . . .

MARIE: Talk to him.

MARTIN: The Doctor.

MARIE: Yeah.

MARTIN: Can I mention your name?

MARIE: Um . . .

MARTIN: Or is not a good idea.

MARIE: Not a good idea.

MARTIN: I completely understand.

(*Pause.*)

    Marie.

MARIE: I know, you're welcome.

MARTIN: No, that's not what I was going to say. I . . .

(*Pause.*)

MARIE: Yeah?

MARTIN: I want to tell you that I feel very . . . *connected* to you right now. And in this world . . . at this *time* . . . that matters.

MARIE: Thank you.

(*Pause. She takes his hand, rests it on the table, and spreads the fingers.*)

You seem tense.

MARTIN: I am. I'm tense.

(*Pause.*)

My plane . . .

MARIE: Sorry?

MARTIN: I, my plane today, it's, we had a nonstandard touch-down.

MARIE: A crash?

MARTIN: No. Not a crash. It's not called a crash. Landing gear wouldn't open. They had to spray the runway with foam so we could slide in.

(*Pause.*)

MARIE: Did anyone die?

MARTIN: No. Actually. I cut my forehead.

MARIE: Were you afraid?

MARTIN: I tried not to be. I tried to *make* myself not . . . I couldn't. Um. Couldn't get away from it. That fear. Of . . . yeah.

(*Pause.*)

At this moment I'm finding myself very attracted to you.

MARIE: Uh-huh.

MARTIN: I've taken a vow of *celibacy* . . .

MARIE: You have.

MARTIN: I just wanted to tell you that.

MARIE: Okay.

(*Pause.*)

> I'm gonna tell *you* a secret, Mister Mirkheim. That nobody knows.

MARTIN: Yes.

MARIE: Why this place is good.

MARTIN: Why?

MARIE: Be quiet. Be very quiet inside yourself. Don't think. Don't look at me. What do you hear?

(*Pause.*)

MARTIN: Nothing. I . . .

(*Pause.*)

> Nothing.

MARIE: That's right.

(*She puts his hand against her forehead.*)

> If you close your eyes? You can feel the strip lights humming.

(*She closes her eyes.* MARTIN *looks at her. Faint humming sound.*)

Scene 6

Hotel desk.

CLERK: Did you enjoy your stay at the Omni Atrium, sir?

MARTIN: Oh yes indeed.

CLERK: Make sure the bill is right, that was the Cattleman
Suite one night, three twenty-eight sixty-five for a double . . .

MARTIN: Single.

CLERK: Pardon?

MARTIN: Single. Just me.

CLERK: Oh. I see.

(Pause.)

I understood you had a guest.

MARTIN: A guest.

CLERK: In the suite. Staying.

(Pause.)

MARTIN: Right. Very good. Just, ah, put it on the card.

CLERK: Yes sir.

MARTIN: She—

CLERK: I understand completely.

(He puts card through phone link.)

MARTIN: Great.

(*Pause.*)

So they watch that lobby, huh?

CLERK: Well, our security's pretty state-of-the-art. We don't want the guests to have any cause for alarm or—

(*Loud beep.*)

Okay. Ah. We're not getting clearance here, sir.

MARTIN: We're not.

CLERK: Uh-uh.

(*Pause.*)

MARTIN: What's that, the—?

CLERK: Visa.

MARTIN: Right. Right, that's the *company's*—here, put it on my personal . . .

(*He takes out another card then quickly puts it back.*)

Tell you what, make it easy, we'll do cash. Not gonna tell me you don't take cash, are you.

CLERK: 'Course we do, sir.

MARTIN (*counting out bills*): Glad to hear it.

CLERK: Sorry about this.

MARTIN: Hey, that's your job. Take it seriously.

CLERK: I do, sir.

MARTIN: I see that. I think it's terrific. I really do.

CLERK: Just trying to get somewhere.

MARTIN: You will, believe me. This is yours.

(*He holds out a twenty-dollar bill.*)

No, come on. Really.

CLERK (*taking it*): Thank you, sir. Have a *very* good trip.

MARTIN: Oh, I'm going to. I know I'm going to. This just absolutely has to be the most incredibly fine day.

(CLERK *turns to register.* MARTIN *looks at credit card.*)

Scene 7

Meeting room. Overhead projector standing next to podium with Rodeway Inn plaque.

Transparency on wall reads:

THE FOUR RULES OF SUCCESS

1. STRENGTH NEEDS NO EXCUSE.
2. THE PAST IS POINTLESS.
3. JUST BECAUSE IT HAPPENED TO YOU DOESN'T MAKE IT INTERESTING.
4. THE THINGS YOU APOLOGIZE FOR ARE THE THINGS YOU WANT.

MARTIN *handcuffed to chair.* SECURITY GUARD, *in suit and tie, sitting opposite. Silence.*

MARTIN: Indian name, isn't it?

GUARD: What.

MARTIN: Minneapolis?

GUARD: American.

MARTIN: One last question.

GUARD: Mmm.

MARTIN: *Are* these necessary?

GUARD: Your behavior made them necessary.

MARTIN: Because you grabbed me. Sir. *You* grabbed *me.* Would you like that? Would you want that *done* to you? Sir?

(*Pause.*)

You're *employed* by Doctor Waxling?

GUARD: I'm employed to protect the security of this motel.

MARTIN: I had a pass.

GUARD: You were asked to leave.

MARTIN: A *pass*, sir.

GUARD: Function was ended.

MARTIN: My flight was late, that's not a crime.

GUARD: Function ends, room's closed.

MARTIN: And that's a law.

GUARD: It's policy.

MARTIN: It's policy. Why are you *keeping* me here?

GUARD: By request.

MARTIN: From whom?

GUARD: Couldn't say.

MARTIN: Sir.

(GUARD *looks at him.*)

We *make* the world. However we choose to act, that's what this world will be. Just consider it.

(GUARD *looks away. Silence.* ROGER *enters.*)

ROGER: Hello.

MARTIN: Hi.

ROGER: Mister Mirkheim, isn't it?

MARTIN: Roger. Good to see you.

ROGER: You like to travel, Mister Mirkheim.

MARTIN: Yes, I do.

ROGER: How did you enjoy Dallas?

MARTIN: *Loved* it. Great city, great people.

ROGER: Took care of your business there?

MARTIN: Mmm-*hmm*.

ROGER: And here you are in Minneapolis.

MARTIN: I am indeed.

(*Pause.*)

ROGER: Now this pass, Mister Mirkheim.

MARTIN: Yes.

ROGER: Obviously I'm *curious* . . . how'd you get it?

MARTIN: Ha.

ROGER: No, but really.

MARTIN: I don't think that matters.

ROGER: You don't.

MARTIN: No.

ROGER: Fair enough.

(*Pause.*)

You're from where'd you say, *Florida*?

MARTIN: That's right.

ROGER: Live in Boca Raton down there, nice town.

MARTIN: Oh yes.

ROGER: Run a booking agency, is it? Various names. You're legally separated from your wife. You were born in Ridgewood, New Jersey. You're not in the film business. You're not talking to any studios. You're not making deals, huh?

MARTIN: Where'd you get this?

ROGER: Just, basically, we can agree on these facts, right?

MARTIN: Who *told* you this?

ROGER: These are just facts, Mister Mirkheim. Very basic facts about a person's life, very easily obtained. Now I bet there are other facts, maybe not quite so easy to find, but nonetheless worthwhile, especially when heard in a court of law.

MARTIN: Okay. We need to stop right here 'cause what you're doing, you're threatening me, that doesn't work.

ROGER: It doesn't.

MARTIN: No, 'cause that's the *past*. You're talking about the past and whatever happened to whoever it was, it's not me. I'm here right now and *that's* me and what *is* at this moment, *that* is what I will deal with. Talk to me about that.

ROGER: I see.

MARTIN: No you don't. You think I'm like you, and the things you're scared of, your reputation, your good *name* or being punished, that's worthless. I know you. I know what you do. You're still afraid your niece'll blab about squeezing Mister Willy.

(*Pause.* ROGER *takes out a small memo book.*)

ROGER (*reading*): 305 673-5400.

MARTIN: What?

ROGER: Florida Bureau of Taxation.

(*Pause.*)

MARTIN: Yes?

ROGER: I think *they* might like to hear about your recent adventures.

MARTIN: What'd you speak to my wife? I have to tell you my wife and I, not to cast, the thing about her, she's, a little bitter, basically she's wasting her life—

ROGER (*starting out*): Mirkheim Enterprises, wasn't it?

MARTIN: Okay.

ROGER: Excuse me?

MARTIN: Okay. What. What.

(*Pause.*)

ROGER: Who gave you the pass, Mister Mirkheim?

(*Pause.*)

MARTIN: The receptionist.

ROGER: Who is that?

MARTIN: In Dallas. Marie.

ROGER: How did that happen, Mister Mirkheim?

MARTIN: It just did.

ROGER: It just *came* upon her to give you this pass.

MARTIN: That is correct.

ROGER: Did you know her? Before?

MARTIN: No.

ROGER: But you know her now.

MARTIN: Yes.

(*Pause.*)

ROGER: Would you excuse me, please?

MARTIN: Right.

(ROGER *exits. Pause. To* GUARD:)

Nice place, Minnesota?

GUARD: I like it.

MARTIN: Bet you're a native, huh.

GUARD: I'm from Baltimore.

MARTIN: What brought you here?

GUARD: Work.

MARTIN: Good. Good for you.

(ROGER *reenters, followed by Doctor* WAXLING.)

ROGER: Mister Mirkheim? This is Doctor Waxling.

MARTIN: Yes, *yes*—

ROGER: He'd like to talk to you.

(ROGER *whispers briefly to* GUARD, *who nods and exits.*)

MARTIN: Yes. Doctor Waxling. I . . . what an honor, sir, what a *great* honor, you have been . . . I wish I could shake your hand, as you can see I'm . . . First *impressions*, huh? This is not . . . there's been a misunderstanding, unfortunately your assistant and I . . . Let me organize my thoughts. I don't want to waste your time or bore you with my problems. The first thing I want, I need to tell you, is what a tremendous influence your work has— I mean drifting through my, my *life*, and you know to look at me, you'd say, "Well he's done pretty—" But *no* because inside what am I, this *fear*, every day that rules us and, I'm talking a lot, all the time afraid to say I don't know *anything*. I DON'T KNOW ANY-THING. Than a *baby*. And what I am, and what I've learned, it's *nothing*. I'm living for *nothing*. And for you

in your work and I watch that show to say, "Yes it's true
and don't pretend, *yes* it's true and *that* will set you
free," has made me strong. In myself. I *believe* in
myself. And for this I just would like to say . . . thank
you.

(*Pause.*)

WAXLING: Did you fuck my woman?

MARTIN: Huh?

WAXLING: That girl, you're fucking her?

MARTIN: I'm sorry, I don't . . .

WAXLING: Roger.

ROGER: Doctor Waxling would like to know if you've had
sexual congress with Marie.

MARTIN: No.

(*Pause.*)

WAXLING: Has he been frisked?

ROGER: Yes sir.

(WAXLING *reaches over, grabs* MARTIN *by the lapels, and
slams his head against a chair.*)

WAXLING: Hey. *Hey.* Do I have your attention?

(MARTIN *nods.*)

Two things people do really rub me the wrong way.
One is *lie*, the other is fuck my women.

MARTIN: Not lying—

WAXLING: What?

MARTIN: I'm not lying, sir—

WAXLING: No no. No. You're fucking with my things, my
things, *mine*, I own them you don't *touch* them I don't
care who you are. I *know* that girl, she has a *low* self-

image, *easily* manipulated, don't think she won't tell me, huh? Everything.

(*Pause.*)

MARTIN: I slept with her.

WAXLING: You did.

MARTIN: Yes.

WAXLING (*grabbing him again*): You greasy little fuck—

MARTIN: That's it. Doctor Waxling. That's *all*.

WAXLING: He *just* screwed her, that's all, guys in fucking *suits*—

MARTIN: I *slept* with her. Just, in the same bed. We slept.

(WAXLING *holds him. Pause.*)

   Like Daniel Strong does. To test himself.

WAXLING: Who?

MARTIN: Daniel Strong. Daniel *Strong*.

(*Pause.*)

WAXLING: You read that, huh.

(MARTIN *nods.*)

   You read my little offering. You had to come see me. Over great distances through hardship to gaze upon my face.

MARTIN: Yes.

(*Pause.*)

WAXLING: Roger.

ROGER: Yes, Doctor.

WAXLING: How many.

ROGER: Well as I explained the print ad mix-up—

WAXLING: How many.

ROGER: Ninety-eight.

WAXLING: How many takers.

ROGER: Now some reason here a lot of Shriners—

WAXLING: How many.

ROGER: Two for the seminar.

WAXLING: Two.

ROGER: Yes.

(*Pause.*)

WAXLING: Where you from?

MARTIN: Boca Raton, it's in Flo—

WAXLING: What time I'm on there?

MARTIN: Three A.M. Sundays.

WAXLING: Oh that's fine. Really splendid. Three A.M., Rodeway Inn, ninety fucking Shriners. I'm doing well. I'm making a *big* noise.

ROGER: The marketing strategy—

WAXLING: They're not *buying* me. I'm not being *perceived.* As a *threat.* I'm not being taken as a threat.

ROGER: I think, when people get scared enough our message—

WAXLING: When's *that* happening, Roger? When are they gonna get *scared*?

ROGER: In *USA Today* a poll showed . . .

WAXLING: Fucking TV my *room* doesn't work . . .

ROGER: . . . homeowners' fear of—I'll have it checked—

WAXLING: Get me something *chocolate.*

(ROGER *looks at* MARTIN, *then exits. Pause.*)

MARTIN: Very often the people who advise us—

WAXLING: No. Don't.

MARTIN: Pardon?

WAXLING: Don't try to impress me with your "thoughts."
Please.

(*Pause.*)

What *is* it with you people, huh?

MARTIN: Who do you mean, Doctor Waxling?

WAXLING: I mean *you people*. Holed up in your ratty little
rooms scribbling on shopping bags. "Now my destiny
seems clear . . . It will all happen today." Not here,
buddy. You're not plugging me in some hotel lobby. I'm
not your double. I'm not sending messages through
your schnauzer. You stay away from *me* and you stay
away from my *things*. What are you, crossing guard or
something? Hospital orderly?

MARTIN: I'm a movie producer.

WAXLING: Are you now.

MARTIN: Yes.

WAXLING: And *not* some obsessional lunatic chasing me
around the country convinced I hold the key to your
life.

MARTIN: No.

WAXLING: Good. 'Cause I catch you fucking with my things
again we don't mess with trespassing, harassment
thirty days of fun. I'll make you disappear. Produce
that.

(*He starts out.*)

MARTIN: I— Could we discuss business?

WAXLING: What?

MARTIN: I came here to discuss business. A business proposition. For you.

(*Pause.*)

WAXLING: Yes?

MARTIN: I believe your book *Daniel Strong* has great com-
mercial potential and I wish to offer you a substantial
sum of money in exchange for the worldwide motion
picture rights.

WAXLING: Uh-*huh*.

MARTIN: Would you be interested in, in such an arrangement?

WAXLING: With you?

MARTIN: Doctor Waxling, I don't blame you for, for— This is
not how I wanted to approach you. This is not accord-
ing to my *plan*. Now you protect yourself. I see that and
I think it's wise. Because, I hope you will allow me to
say this, people aren't listening, they are twisting what
you have to say, they are pushing you down. You of all
people. I know how it is not to be heard. I don't want to
see this happen to you. I would like to bring your
message to millions of people in a simple way they can
understand. And yes I would like to profit by it. I would
like people to know my name. To see my name and
know that I have done something. That I have done
what they could not. That will live on when I am gone.

(*Pause.* WAXLING *takes a bottle of No-Doz and swallows
three or four tablets. He looks at* MARTIN.)

WAXLING: It's basically an adventure story.

MARTIN: And what a story.

WAXLING: It has certain other . . . *elements* . . .

MARTIN: Which affected *me* so—

WAXLING: They trashed it of course.

MARTIN: They didn't understand.

WAXLING: The intel*lec*tuals.

MARTIN: They were scared.

WAXLING: Join their little club.

MARTIN: You were ahead of your time.

WAXLING: The *guardians*. Of *culture*. Our *heritage*. Our precious *heritage*. You know what heritage is?

MARTIN: What?

WAXLING: It's a theme park. With two hundred million personnel managers looking for a salad bar and some fake Elvis in skintights.

MARTIN: Huh.

WAXLING: And me. I'm a voice crying in the Rodeway Inn.

MARTIN: Doctor Waxling. I am here to help you change all that. If you would only let me.

(*Pause.*)

WAXLING: How much are we talking about?

MARTIN: How much . . . ?

WAXLING: Money.

MARTIN: Well . . . the potential, once we get—

WAXLING: No, no. How much will you pay me?

MARTIN: Ah . . . well . . . I wasn't really prepared to get into numbers right—

WAXLING: But just for instance.

MARTIN: How much would you need?

WAXLING: I would need at this moment to live and work in the area of five hundred thousand dollars.

MARTIN: Uh-huh . . .

WAXLING: Half a million the book is yours. You own it, you do what you want.

(*Pause.*)

MARTIN: That could be arranged.

WAXLING: How soon.

MARTIN: Ah, certainly I could advance you a few thousand up front, then when I—

WAXLING: A few thousand.

MARTIN: Yes, of course once it was all in place you'd be seeing—

WAXLING: Where is it now?

MARTIN: Doctor Waxling . . . ah . . . the kind of money you're—

WAXLING: What do you have now? Right now? Quarter of a million? Let's talk. Hundred thousand? Convince me. How much, come on.

(*Pause.*)

MARTIN: I have . . . access to financing.

WAXLING: You have . . . *access*.

MARTIN: Yes, there are certain interested parties—

WAXLING: Give me your wallet.

MARTIN: Huh?

WAXLING: I want your wallet.

MARTIN: I—

WAXLING: Wallet.

(Pause. MARTIN manages to get out wallet with cuffed hands and offers it to WAXLING. WAXLING looks through it, finding only two or three bills inside.)

MARTIN: Doctor Waxling . . . if you tell me what you're looking for, I would . . . I'd be happy to . . . um . . .

(WAXLING looks at MARTIN. Pause.)

What?

(WAXLING keeps staring at him.)

What is it?

WAXLING: This is over.

MARTIN: Doctor Waxling, I am *committed* to—

WAXLING: No, it's alright, really. My fault. I almost took you seriously. You're a nice little tadpole, you shagged my receptionist that's okay.

MARTIN: If you give me some time to, to *structure*—

WAXLING: Oh please. Go *away.* I'm too old for this. There's nothing to talk about.

MARTIN: Please, Doctor Waxling, I *beg* you—

WAXLING: YOU HAVE NOTHING IN YOUR POCKET. You're no kind of threat here. You're no threat at all. Get yourself some money, young man. Go . . . get . . . *money.*

(He throws the wallet at MARTIN.)

Scene 8

On a bus. Day. MARTIN, *asleep. Paperback on seat next to him.* BUS DRIVER, *with plastic trash sack, shaking him.*

DRIVER: Up and at 'em, Johnny. Let's go.

MARTIN: Huh?

DRIVER: All out. Come on. Thank you for choosing Trailways.

(*Pause.*)

MARTIN: What time is it?

DRIVER: Six A.M.

MARTIN: Are we in Miami?

DRIVER: Huh?

MARTIN: This is Miami?

DRIVER: This is Provo.

MARTIN: Can you tell me when we reach Miami?

DRIVER: Lemme see your ticket.

(*Pause.*)

You were supposed to change at K.C.

MARTIN: What?

DRIVER: Miami you had to change at K.C.

(*Pause.*)

MARTIN: I'm where?

DRIVER: Provo. Utah.

(MARTIN *puts his face in hands and starts rocking back and forth.*)

Johnny. Hey Johnny. You okay there? Johnny.

MARTIN: Sorry.

DRIVER: You sick or something?

MARTIN: No.

DRIVER: Somebody you can call?

MARTIN: I don't think so.

(*He stands. Pause.*)

Is it cold in Provo?

DRIVER: Gets cold, yeah. It's cold now.

MARTIN: You're from Utah?

DRIVER: Seattle.

MARTIN: I'm from Florida.

DRIVER: How about that.

MARTIN: I grew up in New Jersey.

DRIVER: It's a big country.

MARTIN: Yes.

(*Pause.*)

DRIVER (*picking up paperback*): This yours?

(MARTIN *doesn't answer.* DRIVER *drops book in sack.*)

Good coffee over the 76 there.

MARTIN: Thank you. Thank you very much.

DRIVER: So you gotta get off the bus, okay?

MARTIN: I will. Certainly.

(*Pause*. DRIVER *walks off.*)

> What am I doing here. What the fuck am I doing here. What the fuck am I doing.

Scene 9

An office. MARTIN *wolfing down sandwich.* KIM *watching him.*

KIM: Some more?

MARTIN: No, I'm, thank you.

KIM: You're sure.

MARTIN: *Uh*-huh.

KIM: Alright.

(*Pause.*)

> So, Martin.

MARTIN: Yes.

KIM: You're not looking your best.

MARTIN: I've been on the road.

KIM: You called me from where?

MARTIN: The Utah region.

KIM: How is it there?

MARTIN: I don't know, Kim. I . . . Cold. It was cold.

KIM: Well, you're in New York now.

MARTIN: Yes.

KIM: How long you here for?

MARTIN: I don't know.

KIM: Where are you staying?

MARTIN: I don't know.

KIM: How is business?

MARTIN: I don't know. I don't have a business. I don't have anything.

(*Pause.*)

KIM: What was it you wanted to see me for, Martin?

MARTIN: Huh?

KIM: When you phoned you said you had to see me.

MARTIN: Yes.

(*Pause.*)

Do you recall our conversation last month?

KIM: On the terrace?

MARTIN: That's right.

KIM: I do indeed.

MARTIN: I felt we made some sort of connection there. That we believed in the same things. That we knew what was important.

KIM: I'm sure that's absolutely true.

MARTIN: I've experienced some . . . setbacks since we last met. My plan failed. I failed. I won't bore you with the details. I met Doctor Waxling. We discussed my proposal at great length and he was very impressed with . . . He couldn't see me as a threat. I didn't present myself as a serious threat and so I failed.

KIM: I regret hearing this.

MARTIN: No. No. It was the best thing that could have happened. Because I'm clean. Now I *know.* It doesn't matter who I am. It doesn't matter what I believe. There's one thing I need. I need to become a threat. I need to become the biggest threat there is. And that's what I'm going to do.

(*Pause.*)

KIM: What was it you wanted to see me for?

MARTIN: I need half a million dollars now. Later I'll need much more.

KIM: Uh-huh.

MARTIN: I don't care how I get it.

KIM: Right.

MARTIN: Do you understand what I'm saying?

KIM: No. I guess I don't.

(*Pause.*)

MARTIN: Kim. You have a *nice* office.

KIM: Thank you.

MARTIN: You make a lot of money, don't you.

KIM: I'm comfortable.

MARTIN: Do you need any help in, in what you do?

KIM: I usually work best alone.

MARTIN: But if someone presented himself to you who was prepared to take risks, would you find a person like that useful?

(*Pause.*)

KIM: You don't know what I do.

MARTIN: I don't care. I mean I do know and it doesn't matter. Whether it's whatever you call it right or wrong, I can't worry about that anymore.

KIM: So this thing that I do, you're saying that you'd like to help me do it, despite its dangers and its possible moral or legal complications?

MARTIN: Yes.

KIM: What is it you think I do?

(*Pause.*)

MARTIN: At the party—

KIM: Which party.

MARTIN: On the *terrace*, they asked you to leave 'cause . . .

KIM: Because why?

MARTIN: Because you . . . you're a dealer. Right? A drug dealer.

(*Pause.*)

Aren't you?

(*Pause.*)

Kim?

(*Pause.*)

KIM: I undertake freelance market analysis for a consortium of Pacific Rim industrial groups.

MARTIN: What?

KIM: Robot systems. Medical equipment. Information retrieval.

MARTIN: No.

KIM: Yes.

MARTIN: No. Oh Jesus. Oh no. God damn it God fucking
damn it. What a fuck-up I am. What a fuck-up loving
asshole. What a shiteating fuckhead. Look at me. Look
at me.

(KIM *looks at him. Pause.*)

Kim. I beg your pardon. I've made some very bad
assumptions about . . . practically everything. And
I . . . Good seeing you. Take care.

(*He starts out.*)

KIM: Martin.

MARTIN: Yes.

KIM: I'd like to offer some advice, if I may.

MARTIN: What?

KIM: There is nothing so valuable in life as a sense of per-
spective.

(*Pause.*)

I am not what you imagined me to be.

MARTIN: I realize that.

KIM: However, I do know members of my peer group who
are. I could arrange for you to meet them. Would you
like that?

MARTIN: Yes.

KIM: Alright.

(*Pause.*)

There are many ways of finding money, Martin. Whatever the climate. Whatever the mood.

MARTIN: This is what has to be done.

KIM: Well, you're a big boy.

(*Pause.*)

You don't smoke.

MARTIN: No.

KIM: I need the nicotine.

(*He takes out a cigarette pack and unwraps it.*)

It's a curious time, isn't it. I find it curious. Curious to be alive. And change . . . change is *hard*. Honestly, *very* hard. Leaving your desk . . . that's hard. We're not free, you know. All of this and we're still not free.

(*Pause.*)

You have faith, don't you.

MARTIN: What?

KIM: Faith.

(*Pause.*)

MARTIN: Yes.

KIM: I envy that.

(*He lights a cigarette and takes a long drag.*)

Yes yes yes. I'm sensing *all* sorts of possibilities.

End Act One.

ACT TWO

Scene 1

A booth in a restaurant. MARTIN *in new suit with* KIM *and* RON.

RON: Miami. Miami. Fucking Miami. Fucking skeeve town. Fucking Cubans. Crazed fucking mothers. I hate fucking Miami. You're not safe in Miami. How the fuck you live there I don't know.

KIM: Martin doesn't live in Miami, Ron.

RON: He doesn't.

MARTIN: No.

RON: Where the fuck *does* he live.

MARTIN: Boca Raton.

RON: Huh. Well. *You* go down there, huh? Kim? You go down Miami, right?

KIM: I sometimes go to Miami.

RON: You're fucking *crazy. New* York. *New* York. *New* York. Last night?

KIM: How was it?

62

RON: The best. The best. Absofuckingwhatley the best. Last
night. Okay. We get there. This is at Shea. We get
there. In the limo. I got, I'm with, the, *Carol*, she does
the, the, *fuck*, you know, that *ad*, the fitness, amazing
bod, amazing bod, fucking amazing bod, and I have, for
this occasion, I put aside my very best, lovely lovely
blow, for Carol, who, no, I care about very deeply. So,
okay, get to Shea, it's fucking *bat* night, everybody with
the bats, fifty thousand bat-wielding sociopaths, security is very tight. *I* have a private booth. In the circle.
This is through GE, my little addictive exec at GE. So
we entrée, me and Carol, and my client, I see, has
fucked me over, 'cause there's already someone there,
you know who, that talk-show guy, he's always got like
three drag queens and a Satanist, and he's there with a
girl can't be more than fourteen. "Oops." This fucking
guy, my *daughter* watches that show. And between us,
heavy substance abuser. I ask him to leave. I mean I
come to watch a ball game with my good friend Carol
and I'm forced to encounter skeevy baby-fucking
cokeheads. One thing leads to the other, politeness out
the window he comes at me Mets ashtray in his hand.
What do I do.

KIM: You have a bat.

RON: I have a bat, I take this bat, I acquaint this individual in
the head with this bat. "Ba-doing." Right, ba-doing?
He doesn't go down. Stands there, walks out the door,
comes back two security guards. "Is there a problem
here, boys?" "Well sir, this man, bicka bicka bicka,"
"Yes, I completely understand and here's something for
your troubles."

KIM: How much?

RON: How much, Kim? How much did I give these good
men to resolve our altercation? I gave them one thousand dollars in U.S. currency. And they were very

grateful. Mister Microphone sits down, doesn't speak, doesn't move rest of the night. Moody fucking person. Mets take it, great ball, home with Carol where we romp in the flower of our youth. I win. I dominate. I get all the marbles. And that is why I love New York.

KIM: Yours is a rich and happy life, Ron.

RON: Yeah, it is, it is so fuck you, you bogus Ivy League skank. You spent four years sucking bongwater at Hofstra just like me. That's a nice suit.

KIM: You like it?

RON: How much you pay for it.

KIM: I paid nothing for this suit, Ron. It was a gift.

RON: Fuck you.

KIM: From an admirer.

RON: Fuck *you*. This fucking guy. You know how many times a week he gets laid?

MARTIN: No.

RON: Neither do I. Ten years since college I know him, butter wouldn't melt. I don't think it's happened. You ever been laid, Kim?

KIM: No, Ron. Never. What's it like.

RON: Fuck you. You get your horn piped by air hostesses every night. You Protestant bastard. That's a nice suit. I don't look good in clothes.

(*Pause.*)

It's hot. Gonna be a hot summer.

(*Pause.*)

What are we here for, so?

KIM: Martin?

MARTIN: I have a proposition for you, Ron.

RON: This is fine. This is wonderful.

MARTIN: First let me say that I'm a person who's comfortable with risk.

RON: Mmm-*hmm.*

MARTIN: And what I want, what I'd like to *present,* to you, is something we might both find very, um, um . . .

KIM: Martin's a businessman, Ron. He understands business. He understands the principles of trust and discretion, and he needs to create some wealth.

(RON *looks at* MARTIN. *Pause.*)

MARTIN: Yes.

(*Pause.*)

RON: Well. This is very nice. This is most lovely for him and I wish him luck. How does he intend to do these things?

KIM: He's going to sell Amway products, Ron. He's going to claw his way to the top of the Amway ladder.

RON: Then fuck *you* with your attitude. I gotta pick up my kid from Dalton twenty minutes, what kind of arrangement you looking for here?

KIM: How are you for blow.

RON: Ooo, "blow," listen to him, "blow," I don't know what you're talking about, I sell landscaping equipment.

KIM: Really.

RON: You know it.

KIM: Well, Martin's interested in putting in a pond.

RON: Hmm, how big a pond?

KIM: How big a pond, Martin?

MARTIN: I . . .

(*Pause.*)

> I've secured an equity loan of two hundred fifty thousand against my property in Florida.

(*Pause.*)

RON: How much?

MARTIN: Two hundred fi—

RON (*to* KIM): I don't find you funny anymore.

KIM: Oh dear.

RON: Fuck you think I am, some TV show?

KIM: No, Ron. You're almost too real.

RON: You fucking bastard.

MARTIN: What's wrong?

KIM: He's considering your offer.

RON: No fucking way.

KIM: Being a little short*sighted*.

RON: No. No. I'm being smart. We're not hello the Palladium six lines in the toilet anymore. The current event, one key a month, close personal friends, I am a happy man. Quarter million, that is, that is, that puts you in a room very close to a bunch of crazed implacable Colombians with enough firepower send you to Venus in pieces.

KIM: Gee, Dad.

RON: Hey, these are *serious people*, Kim. They take one look at no offense Mister Rogers here lunchbox full of cash who is he where's he come from the fuck he's *doing* there anyway he wins a prime chance to lose his nut and sit inside a barrel with his dick shoved up his mouth.

KIM: What a dark view of the world, Ron.

RON: You are such a fucking *tourist*.

KIM: That's me.

RON: It is you, it is *you*. I got your history Kim, you messed with all kindsa wack shit, you took lotsa pictures, but you never rolled the windows down and that has made you one fucked-up little unit.

KIM: This is really not interesting.

RON: 'Cause you never played your *chances*, buddy, you got plenty a toys but you never played your chances.

KIM: I'm playing them now.

RON: Too fucking late, you wanna crash and burn go ahead, *I* operate from a position of safety. I don't know why I let myself be seen with you.

KIM: Because I go out of my way introducing responsible people like this man here—

RON: This man, this man, I don't *know* this man.

KIM: I do. And believe me, let him go you'll regret it.

RON: "Oh."

KIM: Yes. *Yes.* Because someone *else*—

MARTIN: Hold on.

KIM: Someone with vision—

MARTIN: Kim, let me—

KIM: —is going to, just a sec, profit immensely while you're still peddling your little Glad bags—

MARTIN: Kim. *Kim.* Excuse me. I want to *say* something. Alright?

(*Pause.*)

KIM: Please.

MARTIN: Thank you.

(*Pause.*)

> Ron. I'd like to see if I can make you understand my, my purpose in coming here, my goals, what I hope to achieve, and the reasons I feel . . .

(*Pause.*)

> No. No. That's pointless. I want you to *listen* to me. Because this is how it is. There's something I need to get done. I don't have time to waste on . . . *individuals* who won't seize an opportunity. I don't resent them. I don't condemn them. But I will not give them my time.

(*Pause.*)

RON: So?

MARTIN: So here's what you need to know about me. I have a quarter of a million dollars in cash sitting in a briefcase. I'm eager to spend it. Kim has spoken highly of you. You're aware of my proposal. Either on the boat or off, I have to hear now.

RON (*to* KIM): Trying to *threaten* me?

MARTIN: On or off.

RON: "Off." Fuck you. Off.

MARTIN: Fine. Kim, call me? We'll make new arrangements.

KIM: Mmm-hmm.

(MARTIN *gets up and starts out.* RON *looks at* KIM.)

> There you are.

RON: Wait. Wait. Hey. Hey, um, what's his—

KIM: Martin.

RON: Martin. Yo. Martin. Come on. Sit down. Everybody with the attitude. Come on now. Alright.

(*Pause.* MARTIN *returns to the table and sits.*)

MARTIN: Yes?

RON: Wanna be a rich man, huh.

(MARTIN *shakes his head.*)

    Doing this for science?

MARTIN: I'm financing a film.

RON: A film.

MARTIN: A *movie*.

RON: Yeah. Well, um, that makes sense.

MARTIN: I believe it does.

RON: No, I mean, hey, who doesn't go for a little entertainment, right buddy?

KIM: Ron, you've captured the matter in its essence.

(*Pause.*)

RON: I got stuff, I gotta pick up my daughter, I got dry cleaning.

KIM: Righty-o.

RON: This, the thing.

MARTIN: Yes.

RON: I don't know. I'm telling you. I don't know.

MARTIN: What's that mean.

RON: I don't *know.* I'll see what I can *arrange*.

MARTIN: I'm not interested in waiting.

RON: You're not . . . *interested*.

MARTIN: No.

RON: Then fu—

KIM: Ron.

RON: What?

KIM: I consider us friends.

RON: So?

KIM: Do something big with your life. For once.

(*Pause.*)

RON: What's it about.

MARTIN: Huh?

RON: Your movie.

MARTIN: It's based . . .

(*Pause*)

> This creature goes around cracking people's heads open scooping their brains out.

RON: Well. Whatever. I mean I wouldn't take my kid to see it, you know, what *you* laughing about?

KIM: Nothing, Ron.

RON: Hey, rot in hell, you heartless fuck. I'm serious. Try a little compassion, huh, it gets you through the day.

(*Getting up.*)

> Drinks on you.

(*He exits. Pause.*)

KIM: Hungry at all?

MARTIN: God damn it.

KIM: What's the problem.

MARTIN: Why did I do that. Why did I *do* that. I *threw* it away.

KIM: Ah no no no.

MARTIN: I am just so *tired* of little *shits* wasting my time when they can't see past their *own* fear and—

KIM: Martin. You closed this deal. You did. I am very impressed.

MARTIN: Come on.

KIM: Yes. Listen to me. That was perfect with Ron.

MARTIN: Why?

KIM: Because I know him. He's weak and he loves money.

(*Pause.*)

Lesson here for you though.

MARTIN: What.

KIM: Have a little more faith in your own abilities.

(*Pause.*)

MARTIN: I will.

(KIM *looks at menu.*)

Kim.

KIM: Hmm.

MARTIN: What . . . we haven't, what do you want. From this.

KIM: What do you think I should get?

MARTIN: Te— twenty. Twenty percent.

(*Pause.*)

Have I said something wrong?

KIM: No. It's an impressive . . . number.

MARTIN: You deserve it.

KIM: Let me propose something else.

MARTIN: What.

KIM: Partnership.

(*Pause.*)

MARTIN: Kim . . . I . . .

KIM: Want to do it for yourself.

MARTIN: I thought you knew that.

KIM: Yes.

(*Pause.*)

> Most people—I don't mean to be harsh—they have no sense of themselves. They think other people's thoughts. And they waste their lives. That's not for us, Martin. We're better than that and we know it. Now look what we've achieved. Right here at this table, together. I think it's only a start.

MARTIN: Kim. I'm here to get the movie done.

KIM: What happens after that?

MARTIN: I can't think about it now.

KIM: I wish you would. I really wish you would. Because you can make a hundred movies, yes, is that all you came for? You can run a studio, own half of midtown, net four hundred million per, it's only a bigger desk. I've been there Martin believe me please it's *nothing*, nothing at all. But to do what matters, I mean really *do* something out there in the *world* that frees us from this . . . *junk* . . . that's a life. It's the life I read about. It's the life I want. Don't you?

(*Pause.*)

MARTIN: Staying focused . . .

KIM: Yes.

MARTIN: On what's important.

KIM: It's not easy.

MARTIN: No.

KIM: I'll keep you honest.

(*Pause.*)

MARTIN: Alright. I . . . Yes. Alright.

KIM (*lifting his drink*): Well come on then. Let's have an adventure here.

(*They toast.*)

Scene 2

A motel room. MARTIN *with briefcase,* KIM, RON *with kitchen scale,* NUÑEZ *standing by entrance. Silence.*

RON: What is that out there?

KIM: Van Wyck Expressway.

RON: It's like a major fucking highway, huh? Who knew.

KIM: Get out of Manhattan much, Ron?

RON: Hey, you know how many times I been here Ozone Park? Martin?

MARTIN: How many times.

RON: Never. I *never* been to Ozone Park. Looks like fucking *every*place. I never been in a motel room totally skanked as this. Where'd that guy go? It's fifteen fucking minutes.

KIM: Why don't you ask this gentleman?

RON: 'Cause I don't speak *Spanish*.

(NUÑEZ *looks at him.*)

Hi.

(*Pause.*)

KIM: "A boy sat on a bed, wondering who he might turn out to be."

MARTIN: What?

KIM: You know that.

MARTIN: No.

KIM: First line of the book.

MARTIN: It is?

KIM: Look it up.

MARTIN: When this is done I will.

(*Pause.*)

Thank you.

RON: Fuck. Ing. Christ.

(PAMFILO *enters.*)

PAMFILO: Okay. The other car is here.

RON: Terrific.

PAMFILO: They were caught in the traffic from the stadium.

RON: Met game, huh, big Met game today, yeah, uh, you like baseball?

(*Pause.*)

PAMFILO: Who is Ron again?

RON: That's me.

PAMFILO: Okay, I am Pamfilo.

RON: Yeah, right, I know your cousin, we've done business together, I understand he spoke to you, and, ah, how's he doing?

PAMFILO: Eh?

RON: How's your cousin?

PAMFILO: He's good.

(*Pause.*)

RON: Okay. Well. Ah. This, these are my clients, Mister Feston, Mister Mirkheim.

PAMFILO: Yes.

RON: Your cousin met them. Very reliable, dependable gentlemen.

MARTIN: How do you do.

(*Pause.*)

RON: So.

(*Pause.*)

PAMFILO: *¿Los registraste?*

NUÑEZ: *No son nada.*

PAMFILO: *Que te dije, siempre tiene cuidado.* (*To the others:*) Nuñez, he is my . . . security man, okay? He is going to see that everything is safe between us.

(NUÑEZ *frisks* RON, KIM, *and* MARTIN.)

RON: Very sensible.

PAMFILO: Yes. Because sometimes men are not honorable.

KIM: Isn't that unfortunate.

PAMFILO: For them it is.

RON: Ha. Right right right.

PAMFILO: Who is with the money?

MARTIN: Me.

PAMFILO: Yes. May I look please.

(MARTIN *hands him the briefcase.* PAMFILO *opens it but does not look inside.*)

    We have met before.

MARTIN: Pardon?

PAMFILO: You and I.

MARTIN: I don't think so.

PAMFILO: No? Someone who is like you.

MARTIN: Well.

PAMFILO: That's right. The man I am thinking of, he is a good man. He provides for his family and respects the memory of his mother.

MARTIN: Does he.

PAMFILO: Yes. Are you a good man, my friend?

MARTIN: I hope so.

PAMFILO: You're not sure, huh?

MARTIN: I am.

PAMFILO: Then I know you would never try and cheat me.

MARTIN: No.

(*Pause.* PAMFILO *closes the briefcase.*)

PAMFILO (*to* NUÑEZ): *Ve al auto y traeme la bolsa.*

(*To* MARTIN:)

    He is going to bring it.

MARTIN: Great.

(NUÑEZ *exits. Silence.*)

RON: So, what, you live in the city there, Pamfilo?

(*Pause.*)

PAMFILO: No.

(*Pause.*)

    Hempstead.

RON: Out on the Island, huh. That's terrific. Lot a, lot a, lot a Colombians, Hempstead?

PAMFILO: I'm from Honduras.

RON: Say what?

PAMFILO: Honduras. It's a country. It's in America.

(*Pause. Silence.*)

MARTIN: How . . .

PAMFILO: Yes.

MARTIN: How long have you been in, in our land.

PAMFILO: Three years. Since I'm nineteen.

MARTIN: How do you like it.

(*Pause.*)

PAMFILO: You work hard . . . use your head . . . you can be very big.

(KIM *laughs*.)

    That's funny, huh?

RON (*under his breath*): Shut *up*, Kim.

PAMFILO: Hey, you think I'm funny?

MARTIN: Why don't we—

PAMFILO: I'm not so good as you, is that it? Hey.

KIM: No. I'm just enchanted by your optimism. And I sincerely hope that all your dreams come true.

(*Pause.*)

PAMFILO: Thank you.

(NUÑEZ *enters with suitcase.*)

Here is what you want.

(NUÑEZ *hands the suitcase to him. He opens it and displays contents.*)

Okay?

MARTIN: Maybe.

PAMFILO: Try some.

(*He takes out a Saran-wrapped package of coke, opens it, and offers it to* MARTIN. KIM *steps up, reaches into the suitcase and takes out a different package, opens and samples it.*)

KIM: This has possibilities.

PAMFILO: It's what you're looking for, huh.

MARTIN: Means to an end.

PAMFILO: What's that.

MARTIN: This will . . . *get* us . . . where we have to go.

PAMFILO: Yes. I understand.

KIM: I'd like to weigh it.

PAMFILO: It's twelve kilos, what we said.

KIM: I'm sure it is, but . . .

PAMFILO: You don't trust me?

KIM: We just want to weigh it.

(*To* RON:)

Isn't that what they do on TV?

PAMFILO: What. You think I am trying to cheat you?

RON: Hey, *no* one's saying that.

PAMFILO: He's saying it.

RON: Just, we're, a precaution—

PAMFILO (*to* MARTIN): I take you on your honor, my friend, this is how you treat me?

RON: Shit . . .

MARTIN: I'm not doubting—

PAMFILO: This is no good. No. No this is bad business. We don't do it. Here's the money. This is bad, very bad. Nuñez.

(NUÑEZ *starts out.* PAMFILO *follows.*)

MARTIN: Wait. Wait. What do we do . . . ?

RON: Forget about it.

MARTIN: No. Pamfilo. Come on. Let's— We can make this work. We *can.* Kim? Please.

(*Pause.* NUÑEZ *reenters.* PAMFILO *looks at* MARTIN. *He takes suitcase and opens it.*)

PAMFILO: You take one. Whatever one. Take it and weigh it. They all the same. They all a kilo. I don't think like you.

(MARTIN *takes a package from the case. He puts it on the scale.* PAMFILO *looks at* NUÑEZ. *Pause.*)

RON: Two and a quarter, touch under.

PAMFILO: That's a kilo. That's exactly a kilo. Here's another one. Go ahead.

MARTIN: It's alright.

PAMFILO: Go on.

KIM: Make the boy happy, Martin.

MARTIN: Kim. That's enough.

(*Pause.*)

Pamfilo. My apologies. Please.

(PAMFILO *looks at* MARTIN, *closes suitcase and offers it to him.* MARTIN *takes it. He hands* PAMFILO *the money.*)

PAMFILO: *Este payaso no sabe ni papa.*

MARTIN: What?

PAMFILO: Always know your friends.

(*He exits with* NUÑEZ. MARTIN *takes package off scale, puts it back in case, and shuts it.*)

KIM: Well.

MARTIN: Right.

KIM (*offering his hand*): We're in it now.

(*Pause.*)

MARTIN (*taking it*): Yes.

KIM: No. We're *in* it. We're really *in* it. *Everything's* going to happen.

MARTIN: One less thing in the way.

(KIM *sees* RON *staring at the floor.*)

KIM: Something on your mind, Ron?

RON: Yeah. Let's give me my cut and get the fuck out of here as rapidly as possible.

Scene 3

A rec room. MARTIN, KIM *with briefcase. Late.*

MARTIN: How do you know this guy?

KIM: Shared a house one summer. He was doing three grams a day.

(*Pause.*)

MARTIN: I grew up around here.

KIM: Did you.

MARTIN: My parents bought a place. Paid cash. Big moment
for them. Saved up, fourteen years. Nineteen sixty-
eight.

KIM: Ancient times.

MARTIN: Yeah.

(*Pause.*)

This afternoon, Kim. The motel.

KIM: Mmm-hmm.

MARTIN: Don't act that way again. Okay?

KIM: Why not.

MARTIN: I don't like it.

(*Pause.*)

We have to agree what we're doing stays normal. I am
calling it business and that's how I need it be.

KIM: You're just tired.

MARTIN: It's how I need it, Kim.

KIM: I have a business, Martin. It's in an office. I'm there
every day. We discussed something else.

MARTIN: That was talking. This has to get *done*. I cannot
afford any risks. Do we understand each other?

(*Pause.*)

Kim. Do we—

LEE (*entering*): Sorry. Had to switch the security system
back on. Press the wrong button I get the Short Hills
police force storming the pool deck.

KIM: Can't be too safe.

LEE: You can't, you can't. Kim, get you a drink? Marvin?

MARTIN: Martin. No thank you, Lee.

LEE: Fair enough. Serious man. Welcome to New Jersey. You guys have trouble getting here?

KIM: No.

LEE: Hit traffic?

MARTIN: Not this time of night.

LEE: Yeah. Look. I apologize for that. My schedule's been, you don't wanna know, I'm not even getting home till eleven. I don't see my wife, the twins, forget it.

KIM: Working you hard, huh, Lee.

LEE: Sucking me dry, Kim. But it's worth it. We want early breakfast. We want name recognition before the primaries. 'Cause the momentum is there. Uh. Uh. Organization is there. Money's there. We're jumping straight into the grown-up pool. Really. I mean this one counts, and, uh, uh . . .

(*Pause.*)

    Yeah, I'm sorry, what was I saying?

MARTIN: Something that counts.

LEE: Right, exactly.

KIM: Lee's consulting for Paul Kinsen.

MARTIN: Who?

LEE: Senator Kinsen. Arizona.

MARTIN: You consult on . . . ?

LEE: Chief of media relations actually. Got the whole campaign.

KIM: Congratulations.

LEE: And all I had to do was blow him.

MARTIN: Excuse me?

LEE: I'm kidding of course. Great opportunity for me, something *big*.

KIM: Old Mister Stars and Jackboots.

LEE: What are you, some pansy Democrat?

KIM: I'm a registered bystander.

LEE: Look at Kinsen this year. Try Kinsen out. Kinsen could be very very good for you.

KIM: Why's that.

LEE: 'Cause he wants to win and he's primed to kick ass.

KIM: I'm loving it.

LEE: Which is what I'm saying. He's the man for the nineties. He's rancho samurai. Okay, story: I'm out there, on his "land," this is cactus, cows, he's talking about saddles, this snake, I'm serious, shoots up, I'm like whoa, this is *real*, boom he's on it with the boots stomping its brains out. And that sucker *died*. You get the pitch? Here's a killer. Here's a guy ready for anything. Here is a man who does not know fear. Is that what you want in a Great White Father? I think so. Check this out, what do you think, dummy ad, national spot, wanna hear it, okay, great.

(*He picks up a stack of storyboards.*)

What it is, should be, is a *movie*, a little thirty-second movie about something we want to say. Very simple, morning light, very clean, very "American." Uh, uh, uh, young boy, blond hair, big horse. Tries to climb on. Can't. Falls off. Hits hard. Eats dirt. You with me?

MARTIN: Yes.

LEE: Voice-over: "There are some who believe the best is behind us. Some who think we've lost the way. Some who feel that fear rules the length and breadth of a once proud land." Dramatic Pause. Kid stands up. Tight on the face. V.O.: "Paul Kinsen believes differently. He believes in a nation whose future means more than its past. He believes in a nation unafraid of its strength. He believes in a nation of dreams. Because dreams can be real." Kid slaps the dust off. Beat. "If we want them to be." Kid grabs the stirrup, whatever. He's up. He's on. He's riding. He's a winner. *And* dissolve to Kinsen, presidential as hell. Super-titles: "Paul Kinsen. Believe . . . the . . . what." Believe the *what,* huh. Believe the something. What's good to believe in.

MARTIN: Are you asking me?

LEE: I'm stuck at the tag. Breaking my balls Kinsen this fucking presentation. Know what he's saying? "Why can't it be me on a horse?" I mean I'm on the team ten thousand percent but Wonder Chimp the man isn't, please, I didn't say that. What do we believe in here, *I* don't know, I don't, I honestly don't, no idea. Boom boom boom.

MARTIN: How about possibilities.

LEE: Huh?

MARTIN: Believe the possibilities. We all believe in possibilities, don't we, keeps us going.

LEE: "Believe the Possibilities."

MARTIN: You got it.

KIM: That's amusing, Martin.

LEE: "Paul Kinsen: Believe the Possibilities." Yum dum dum ba dum bum ba bum bum. Hell does that mean.

MARTIN: What do you think it means?

LEE: It means, I don't know, Go for the Gusto, Be All You Can Be, Ram Tough, it means whatever you want it to mean, it doesn't mean anything, it sounds good. Am I right? Is that it? Hello?

(*Pause.*)

MARTIN: Yes. That's it exactly.

LEE (*to* KIM): What flew up his ass?

KIM: Past his bedtime.

MARTIN: I'm fine.

KIM: You'd better be, friend.

(*They look at each other.* MARTIN *turns away.*)

MARTIN: Let's get down to business.

LEE: *Yes.*

MARTIN: This has to be a cash—

KIM: *Mar*tin and I have something very special here, Lee. I want you to *know* you're the first person we thought of.

LEE: Thank you. I'm excited.

KIM: You should be.

LEE: Little *surprised* . . .

KIM: Why's that.

LEE: I didn't know you were dealing.

KIM: Disappointed?

LEE: Well, you know. It's a step. It's a gray area.

KIM: I like me in gray.

LEE: Yeah, right. Boom boom boom.

MARTIN: We discussed possibly a couple of kilos.

LEE: Well, a couple, one, I'm getting off it, but if the quality—

MARTIN: The quality is superb.

LEE: 'Cause what I *been* buying—

KIM: We hear you.

LEE: It doesn't really get me, it just doesn't seem to get me as, it doesn't seem to *give* me the same feeling of . . .

KIM: Uh-huh.

LEE: The same, uh, uh, uh . . .

MARTIN: Strength.

LEE: Yeah. Strength. Strength. Yeah. Yeah.

(*Pause.*)

And I won't fuck with crack, you know. I won't. 'Cause that's really, that is a very *bad*, um . . . problem.

KIM: Then Lee, absolutely is this for you.

(*He takes a kilo bag out of the briefcase and lays it before* LEE.)

Look at that.

LEE: Hmm.

KIM: Shines just like mica.

LEE: Yeah, this could be good for me.

KIM: I think so.

LEE: 'Cause I *need* it.

KIM: Go ahead.

(LEE *tries some. Pause.*)

What did I tell you?

(LEE *says nothing.*)

Now I want you to know that there is plenty more if—

LEE: What are you doing here, Kim?

KIM: Excuse me?

LEE: I don't, is this a joke?

KIM: No.

MARTIN: What's the problem?

LEE: This is garbage.

KIM: No. I've *tried* it, Lee.

LEE: You have?

KIM: Yes, and it's the best coke you can—

LEE: Bullshit.

KIM: Lee—

LEE: *Bull*shit. This is what you buy outside the Port Authority before you catch the bus. I'm past this, I'm *way* past it, you think you're gonna fool me?

(*Pause.* KIM *tries some.*)

MARTIN: What's happening, Kim?

KIM: Hold on a second.

LEE: This won't even get my *tongue* high.

KIM: Give me a *second*, Lee.

LEE: Asking for big money you better—

KIM: Shut up. Lee, okay.

LEE: Hey, this is my *house*, buddy, you don't speak to me—

MARTIN: Kim—

KIM: YES, GIVE ME ONE *SECOND* PLEASE THANK YOU.

(*Pause.*)

Cases.

MARTIN: What?

KIM: The motel. They switched cases.

MARTIN: I don't—

KIM: They *switched cases*. They forced the *argument*, he *stepped* into the hall, they came back we weighed the kilo—

MARTIN: No.

LEE: Hey, you wanna keep it down—

KIM: They took us.

MARTIN: No. No.

KIM: We *sucked* it up—

MARTIN: But they, he offered—

KIM: Stupid *white* boys and they *took* us.

MARTIN: No. No. There's a deal. You— We have a *deal*. You're gonna buy this.

LEE: Keep dreaming.

MARTIN: You're buying. God *damn* you. You have to *buy*—

(TERRY, *Lee's wife, enters in robe.*)

LEE: Don't threaten me, Pee Wee, I don't buy jack from you, hi honey, are we too loud?

TERRY: What's going on . . . ?

LEE: Hon, ah, you remember Kim Feston from the *summer*.

TERRY: . . . half awake and I, hello . . .

KIM: How are the twins, Terry.

TERRY: Oh, they're . . .

LEE: Kim and his friend are very interested in fund-raising for Senator Kinsen, we're just connecting on it, they want to help us along see if they can make a difference.

TERRY: It's late, Lee. You're never going to get up.

LEE: I know, I'll, in a minute. Really.

(*Pause.*)

TERRY: Anybody want tea?

LEE: No sweetie, thank you.

(*Pause.*)

TERRY: Well, come to bed soon.

(LEE *nods. She exits. Pause.*)

MARTIN: I'm fucked. I am fucked. What have I done.

LEE: Excuse me. Over here. This is *my* rec room you're sitting in. I got a wife and two baby kids upstairs, I got a presentation due nine o'clock in the morning, and I have NO FUCKING WAY of getting high tonight. So would you please leave.

KIM: Lee, I suggest—

LEE: You have nothing to say to me, Kim. You just went belly-up.

Scene 4

A car. MARTIN. KIM *behind the wheel. Silence.*

MARTIN: That was the turnoff.

KIM: What?

MARTIN: That was the turnoff for New York.

(*Pause.*)

KIM: I'll take the next exit.

MARTIN: Yah.

KIM: We'll turn around.

MARTIN: 'Kay.

(*Pause.*)

I'm fucked, Kim.

KIM: Stop it.

MARTIN: I am. I'm *fucked.* I'm *so* fucked.

KIM: That's not *helping,* alright.

MARTIN: You don't understand the position—

KIM: We had a setback. We were too eager. We made a mistake, that's done. We move on.

MARTIN: Where. Where do we move *to.*

KIM: We can sell the coke. It's a garbage cut but we can sell it.

MARTIN: For how much?

KIM: Less.

MARTIN: To who?

KIM: Somebody stupid.

MARTIN: Who?

KIM: I have to think about it.

MARTIN: You don't *know.*

KIM: I have to *think.* I have to work it *out.*

MARTIN: Do you know what you're doing, Kim? Do you? I really need to find out. Do you have any *idea*?

KIM: There's always possibilities.

MARTIN: The *money*—

KIM: You don't care about money.

MARTIN: But *my* money, Kim. That was *my*— I mean it was a
loan. You *know* that. I can't pay that back. I was counting on the, the . . . I don't *have* it. You understand?
Anywhere. I'm *already* . . . Here it is. Okay. I've been
bad about money. I've been really *bad*. I'm in a, a,
situation with it and I don't see how I can get out. It's
going to bury me, Kim. I'm really afraid it's going to
bury me and—

(*Rotating lights of a squad car start flashing behind them.*)

Oh fuck.

KIM: It's alright.

MARTIN: What's happening?

KIM: I don't know.

MARTIN: Were we speeding?

KIM: We'll find out.

MARTIN: It's not us, I'm sure it's not, don't stop, what are you
doing—

KIM: Hide the briefcase, would you, Martin.

MARTIN: What?

KIM (*pulling car over*): Hide the briefcase please. Under the
seat.

MARTIN: This is not me. This is not where I'm supposed to
be . . .

KIM: It would be a good idea to hurry up right now.

MARTIN: It won't *fit*.

KIM: I'm sure it will.

MARTIN (*trying to jam it under*): It won't. It won't. Oh fuck what am I doing here.

KIM: Martin. Stop it. Stop it. Alright. It's just a briefcase. Everybody has one.

(STATE TROOPER *approaches with nightstick-style flashlight in hand.*)

There is absolutely nothing to get alarmed about.

(TROOPER *comes up to driver's side.*)

Officer.

TROOPER: Posted speed limit on this parkway is fifty-five miles an hour.

KIM: Yes.

TROOPER: You're clocked on radar at seventy-six.

KIM: Yes. Of course.

TROOPER: See your license, please.

KIM: Certainly.

(TROOPER *inspects license. Pause.*)

MARTIN: Just got a little lost on our way back to the city.

TROOPER: Which city is that.

MARTIN: New York.

TROOPER: I've heard of it.

MARTIN: Right. Ha.

KIM: Officer, it's late, I understand the violation, please, we'll just take the ticket.

TROOPER: Rushing off to bed, huh.

MARTIN: We have a big presentation to make first thing in the morning.

TROOPER: Do you.

MARTIN: Yes.

TROOPER: Back there in New York.

MARTIN: That's correct.

(TROOPER *shines light into car. Briefcase is on Martin's lap. He looks straight ahead at nothing.*)

KIM: I tell you, next time I set the cruise control and forget about it.

(*Pause.*)

    You know?

MARTIN: What?

KIM (*to* TROOPER): Creeps up on you, check the speedometer, and—

TROOPER: Could you both step out of the car please?

MARTIN: What for?

TROOPER: I'm asking you to.

KIM: Is this really necessary?

TROOPER: If you want it to be.

(*Pause.*)

KIM: Fine. Let me turn the engine off.

TROOPER: Uh-huh.

(KIM *shuts off engine and drops the keys.*)

KIM: Great.

(*Hunching over.*)

    I dropped my keys. I'm sorry. Could you just shine your light here? One sec.

TROOPER (*leaning in*): Where.

KIM: Right here.

(*Coming up.*)

   Okay. I found them.

(*He has a small-caliber pistol in his hand.*)

MARTIN: Kim, are you—?

(KIM *grabs the flashlight and shoots the* TROOPER *point-blank in the face. Pause.*)

KIM: Look what I've done.

Scene 5

A field by a road. MARTIN *with Trooper's flashlight,* KIM *smoking cigarette.*

KIM: Where are we?

MARTIN: I don't know.

KIM: I thought you were from New Jersey.

MARTIN: Not this part.

KIM: Sky's lit up in that direction.

MARTIN: It's a refinery. They're all up and down here. We should have stayed on the parkway.

KIM: You might want to shut that off.

(MARTIN *shuts off flashlight. Pause.*)

MARTIN: What are we going to do.

KIM: I'm going to enjoy this cigarette.

MARTIN: Why didn't you tell me Kim.

KIM: You know I've been afraid, I'll say it now, really afraid.
Afraid to be *tested*. Afraid I wouldn't be strong. But I
was. I *was*. You *saw* that I was, God I feel—

MARTIN: Kim, you should have *told* me.

KIM: What did you want to know, I was *ready,* he stood
there and— look how this hand's shaking—

MARTIN: That you had a *gun*, a fucking *gun*.

KIM: Can't have an adventure without a gun.

MARTIN: Fuck adventure this was my *business*.

KIM: Whatever you want to call it.

MARTIN: No Kim, no, my *business* we were conducting, not
some, some, in the street that you read about, a guy,
some bracelet he gets . . . *shot* Jesus *Christ* there's
blood on my shirt.

KIM: Would you rather be arrested?

MARTIN: I don't know.

KIM: You must have an *opinion*.

MARTIN: I DON'T KNOW. MY BRAIN'S GONE AND I
CAN'T *THINK* ANYMORE.

(*Pause.*)

KIM: Let me tell you something, Martin. It might help you,
because it's true. Everything . . . *everything* up to this
exact moment . . . is the Past. We're done with it.
You're concerned about that policeman? I am not. It's
so clear to me. What did he want to do? Take what we
have and punish us. By whose authority? Not mine,

Martin. Not mine. This is so *clear* now. It's a dead little planet we're standing on. I'm alive. And I don't need to be forgiven one goddamn thing. Do you?

(*Pause.*)

Now we have several possibilities spread before us. We can go on debating ethics in the middle of a marsh. We can ease up to the next state trooper and turn ourselves in. Or we can drive back to Manhattan, secure in the knowledge that we are two polite young white men in well-cut suits and will . . . not . . . be . . . touched. Because we set the standards. And we judge *ourselves* accordingly.

(*Pause.*)

It's freedom, Martin. I am talking to you about being free.

(*Pause.*)

MARTIN: I'm done.

KIM: What's that mean.

MARTIN: I'm finished with it.

KIM: Just like that.

MARTIN: Yes.

KIM: I thought you wanted to be a threat.

MARTIN: I don't know what I "wanted to *be.*" I can't *remember.* I've eaten myself up and there's nothing left. *Nothing*.

KIM: You're very weak. Aren't you.

MARTIN: I *am,* so fuck it. Fuck the coke. Fuck the money, fuck *all* money. And fuck the movie. I won't make it. Who was I kidding. It's shit anyway—

KIM: Is it.

MARTIN: *Yes,* let's say it, that book is just *shit.* Some fucking fantasy about power and, and, "everything is possible." Where *are* they, where are these "possibilities," I don't see them, *this* is it, this is life and that's ALL IT WILL EVER BE.

KIM: Where are you going, Martin.

MARTIN: To find the highway. Let go of me.

KIM: That's a bad idea, Martin.

(MARTIN *keeps walking.*)

   Martin. This is your mess.

MARTIN: Fuck it.

KIM: Your *mess,* Martin, I won't get stuck with it . . .

(MARTIN *keeps walking.*)

   Hey. You. Little man.

(*He takes out the gun and shoots, hitting* MARTIN *in the leg.* MARTIN *shouts and falls.* KIM *starts toward him.*)

KIM: I *bet* that hurts, huh.

MARTIN: You bastard . . . we're *part*ners . . .

KIM: You just changed that, didn't you.

(*He reaches* MARTIN.)

   Finish what you start.

(*He puts the gun against Martin's head.*)

MARTIN: Kim. Please.

KIM: Hmm.

MARTIN: I can't face it, I can't, I can't, I'm scared, I'm so scared . . .

KIM: I'm sorry for you.

(*He pulls the trigger. Gun jams. Pause.*)

Would you give me that?

MARTIN: What?

KIM: Give me the flashlight please?

MARTIN: No . . .

KIM: Come on.

MARTIN: HELP ME! SOMEBODY HELP ME!

KIM: Shh. Quiet. Don't be frightened.

MARTIN: *Fuck* you . . .

KIM: Yes, alright. Just give me the flashlight. Come on. You know you're not up to this. Give me the flashlight everything will be okay. Nothing to get alarmed about. You're safe. You are. You really are.

(*Pause.*)

MARTIN: Here.

(*He butts* KIM *in the face with the flashlight.* KIM *staggers back.* MARTIN *clubs him again, swinging wildly.*)

You *want* this? You *want* it? Take it, *take* it!

KIM: Martin— Okay—

MARTIN: HERE'S YOUR THREAT.

KIM (*collapsing*): Uh—

MARTIN: HERE'S YOUR POSSIBLE. HERE'S YOUR SAFETY, YOU FEEL THAT?

(KIM *stops moving.* MARTIN *keeps beating him.*)

GET UP. GET UP. I'M READY. I AM NOT AFRAID. I AM NOT AFRAID.

(KIM *lies face down.* MARTIN *lowers his arms. Long pause.*)

Kim. Hey. Look at this. Look at it, you fuck.

(*He pushes* KIM *over with his foot and displays the flashlight barrel.*)

That's your blood. You see it? That's *your* blood. Here's what I know. I'm stronger than you.

Scene 6

RADIO ANNOUNCER (*voice-over in blackout*): . . . In local Jersey news, police are pursuing what they call "several promising leads" in last week's brutal slaying of Officer Thomas Selby, an eight-year veteran of the highway patrol. Selby was shot point-blank in the face when he stopped a motorist just south of the Irvington exit on the Garden State. He will be buried with full honors tomorrow. In a separate incident, investigators are still hoping to identify the body of a man found bludgeoned to death near the Linden refinery fields Wednesday morning. The man was described as white, well dressed, approximately thirty years old. Police are considering the possibility that the murder was drug-related. They have no leads at this time.

Scene 7

An office. Bright sun. MARTIN *behind a big desk. He stares into space.*

CARLING (*entering, with briefcase*): Mister Powers?

(*Pause.*)

   Mister Powers.

MARTIN: Yes. Come in. Mister Carling.

CARLING: That's right.

MARTIN: Glad to meet you. Welcome to California.

CARLING: Thank you.

MARTIN: Bet you don't get out here much.

CARLING: First time.

MARTIN: Well. Happy New Year. Make way for tomorrow, huh?

CARLING: Ready or not.

(*Pause. He notices poster.*)

   That one of yours?

MARTIN: Oh yes.

CARLING: *Dead World.*

MARTIN: Buckets-of-blood quickie. Did for half a million and it looks it. Got us started though.

CARLING: Huh.

MARTIN: We're doing a big one now. Big picture. Very proud of it. Shooting it down in Mexico, great facilities there. Lovely people. It's all much easier in Mexico.

CARLING: What is it.

MARTIN: Called *Daniel Strong,* based on a book, ah, wonderful wonderful story, about a little guy overcomes all the odds to make his dream a reality. It's upbeat, it's about winners, and, uh . . . it'll be great.

CARLING: And you don't have to be down there for that.

MARTIN: Wish I could. Tell you the truth, I'd rather watch my son play softball. You have children, Mr. Carling?

CARLING: Afraid not.

MARTIN: It changes you. It truly changes you.

(*Pause.*)

CARLING: Mister Powers, I think you know we have a problem.

MARTIN: We seem to, and I thank you for getting in touch with me.

CARLING: Certain evidence has come into my possession that links you to Mister Martin Mirkheim, the subject of my investigation.

MARTIN: What evidence is that.

CARLING: It arises out of a lawsuit brought against Far Horizon Films, I believe that's your company, by a Doctor Waxling, for nonpayment and breach of contract.

MARTIN: Mirkheim.

CARLING: That's right.

MARTIN: Don't know who you're talking about.

(*Pause.*)

CARLING: Mister Powers. You should be aware that I'm authorized to start extradition proceedings. If my conclusions warrant it.

MARTIN: Of course.

CARLING: Tax evasion is a serious crime and the state of Florida will vigorously pursue prosecution.

MARTIN: As well they should.

CARLING: I hoped my visit here would give you an opportunity to come to terms with your situation.

MARTIN: Yes, you mentioned that on the phone. I'm not sure what your point is.

CARLING: My point . . . is that back taxes are the least of Mr. Mirkheim's concerns.

(*He produces a file folder from his briefcase.*)

You might want to read this. Just bits and pieces, you'd have to fit them together. Takes a little time. But I happen to be curious about the past.

MARTIN: I prefer the future.

CARLING: Well. At this moment, our future is what we make of it. I'd say.

(*Pause.*)

MARTIN: You know, I have something here for you.

CARLING: Really.

MARTIN: Yes. I think you dropped it when you came in.

(*He reaches into desk drawer and brings out a thick envelope.*)

CARLING: That's possible.

MARTIN (*sliding envelope across desk*): Check inside to be sure. Go ahead.

(CARLING *opens envelope and looks inside.*)

CARLING: This *is* mine. Thank you.

MARTIN: Don't mention it. I hate losing things.

(*He reaches back into the drawer and brings out a pistol, placing it casually on the desk. Pause.*)

CARLING: Mister Powers, I'm . . . sorry to have taken up your time.

MARTIN: Look, I hope you find the guy.

CARLING: We'll see. It's an easy country to disappear in.

(*He rises, still holding file folder.*)

MARTIN: That stays.

CARLING: Of course.

(CARLING *places file folder on the corner of the desk and exits.* MARTIN *watches him go. Pause. He presses a button on the speakerphone.*)

MARTIN: Nothing till I buzz please.

(*He brings the folder before him and opens it. He thumbs through the pages, looking them over, then returns to the beginning.*)

(*Pause.*)

(*He begins to methodically tear each page into narrow strips.*)

Lights begin to fade.

(MARTIN *continues tearing, increasing speed as he works through the file. The strips pile up on the desk around him.*)

Lights to black.

End